George Charles Smith
of Penzance

The Reverend George Charles Smith (1782–1863).
(Courtesy of The Sailors' Society)

George Charles Smith of Penzance

FROM NELSON SAILOR TO MISSION PIONEER

Roald Kverndal

WILLIAM CAREY
LIBRARY

Wisdom, it is said, is often best taught by experience. In the case of "Boatswain Smith," he gained the wisdom to become the worldwide grandfather of Christian ministry among seafarers by himself "coming up through the hawse pipe." The author has knitted together a fascinating series of vignettes from Smith's own words into the inspirational life story of a man of extraordinary vision and faith.

MONSIGNOR JAMES E. DILLENBURG,
FORMERLY INTERNATIONAL SECRETARY OF THE APOSTLESHIP OF THE SEA
AT THE VATICAN

This book is a tremendous treasure. Tracing the life of the founder and fearless advocate of ministry among People of the Sea, the book belongs to the practical theology of seafarers' chaplains everywhere. It can also serve as a wonderful challenge to seafarers themselves to minister among their own. When I recently shared a glimpse of this Pioneer Pastor from Penzance with a seafaring friend of mine, he was just all ears and begged me for a copy one day.

REVEREND PETER IBRAHIM,
VETERAN PORT CHAPLAIN TO INTERNATIONAL SEAFARERS IN HAMBURG

Ever since George Charles Smith received his original call to seafarers' mission in the early 1800s, he has been an icon and inspirer for others—across all denominational boundaries. I too have been greatly indebted to him—not least during my many years of service in the Norwegian Seamen's Church in London, as a direct successor to Smith's groundbreaking ministry in the Danish-Norwegian Temple there. Dr. Roald Kverndal deserves our thanks for researching the life story of this truly heroic pioneer.

REVEREND DAGFINN KVALE,
THIRTY-YEAR CHAPLAIN IN THE NORWEGIAN SEAMEN'S MISSION

George Charles Smith of Penzance: From Nelson Sailor to Mission Pioneer

Copyright © 2012 by Roald Kverndal

Published by William Carey Library
1605 E. Elizabeth Street
Pasadena, CA 91104 | www.missionbooks.org

Produced in affiliation with the International Association for the Study of Maritime Mission (IASMM)

Melissa Hicks, editor
David Shaver Sr., content editor
Kate Hegland, copyeditor
Josie Leung, graphic design
Rose Lee-Norman, indexer

Cover art courtesy of the National Maritime Museum of Greenwich, London (NMM Image PW 5874). Title: "The *Agamemnon* cuts out French vessels from Port Maurice, near Oneglia, 1 June 1796." This contemporary painting by Nicholas Pocock shows the sixty-four gun HMS *Agamemnon* in action, described by the National Maritime Museum, as "Nelson's favourite ship" that he commanded as captain. It was on this vessel that George Charles Smith would come to serve from 1797 to 1802.

William Carey Library is a ministry of the
U.S. Center for World Mission
Pasadena, CA | www.uscwm.org
Printed in the United States of America

16 15 14 13 12   5 4 3 2 1 BP700

Library of Congress Cataloging-in-Publication Data

Kverndal, Roald.

George Charles Smith of Penzance: From Nelson Sailor to Mission Pioneer/ Roald Kverndal.

p. cm.

Includes bibliographical references and index.

ISBN 978-0-87808-394-7

1. Smith, George Charles, 1782-1863. 2. Merchant mariners--Missions and charities--England--History--19th century. I. William Carey Library. II.
Title.

BV2678.S65K84 2011

266.0092--dc23

[B]

2011026894

IN HONOR OF ALL PEOPLE OF THE SEA

PAST–PRESENT–FUTURE

CONTENTS

FOREWORD

I am thrilled by what I read in this book, about a man of God who troubled the church by always "living on the edge." As Roald Kverndal observes in his preface, "Smith was passionate in his rejection of discrimination relating to the most marginalized." At the same time, I am genuinely humbled as I realize that I am, in my present ministry, literally "following in his footsteps."

There is much to learn from George Charles Smith and the work to which the Lord clearly called him. Readers will be especially impressed by the enduring importance this man placed on the souls of seafarers. Just over two hundred years since Smith's memorable encounter in Penzance, with a couple of seafarers belonging to the revenue cutter *Dolphin*, those of us who in our day minister among mariners and their dependents may well be tempted to overlook their greatest peril. While it was widely affirmed that Smith was essentially a good man, we discover in these pages that, for his part, he would have rejected such an epitaph. George Charles Smith was first and foremost a "gospel man."

The events which took place in the town of Reading on March 19, 1803—a time when Smith believed he was close to death—involved the gentle witness of a nurse, the effect of a sermon he overheard, and the personal attention of "many pious men." All he would later do in the seafaring world would be shaped by what the Lord had done for his soul that day in Reading.

I have found this man so difficult to define, whether in relation to his pastoral ministry in Penzance or his maritime mission in the Port of London and elsewhere. But regardless of the context, his achievements in life became fundamentally impacted by what took place in Reading. Whatever else he was or was not, George Charles Smith was above all a preacher of the gospel. And the greater his love for the gospel, the more inventive he became in determining where and how he could gather people to hear it. As Smith wrestled with God for an "open door for preaching the gospel to the poor," I make a guess that he was as surprised as many who would follow him to find this "open door" at the top of a gangway and not at the end of a garden path!

It was not until 1812, when Smith preached his first sermon to sailors at the Carter Lane Chapel, that opportunities for preaching to mariners as such were fully realized. Encouraged by posters and fliers sent to the ships, and guided by torch bearers in the streets, seafarers converged at this chapel, situated in the most notorious sector of London's "Sailor Town." Here he preached with such power and conviction that "hundreds of sailors were in tears." Soon it was the iconic "Bethel Flag" that would invite sailors to share the gospel on board ships at anchor and enjoy fellowship with one another. Aware as he was of all the temptations abounding on either shore of the river, Smith readily joined them and said he counted it "an honour to stand among them and mingle his prayers and praises with theirs."

The intricate details which Kverndal brings to his canvas give us as full a picture as is possible of George Charles Smith—a man of God as flawed as he was faithful and as vilified as he was victorious. He probably lacked all the necessary characteristics of what we would today call a "team player" and leaves me in no doubt that his individualism was as personally destructive as it was publically daring.

With me, you will read of the *London Ark*, of William Wilberforce, of the Port of London Society, of the collier brig *Zephyr*, of the Bethel Seamen's Union, of *The Sailor's Magazine*, and of globalization, prostitutes, and orphans. Kverndal peels back the layers of history as he shows the struggles between newly founded maritime mission societies, while revealing the heart of a man who was not wanted by many and yet welcomed by far more.

Foreword

I like this man, a much-needed nuisance sadly missing from the maritime canvas of our own day. At the same time, I am troubled by this man, who was as much a prophet as he was a preacher, whose faith and focus still ask questions of us today. In order to accept him and prize his ministry as greatly as I do, it has become necessary to embrace him in full. If he is, as I agree, the founder of the Modern Maritime Mission Movement, then we need to reflect on what it was he founded and judge our proximity to his pattern.

I welcome this third publication by Kverndal and pray that it may be used by God, especially among those of us who have been blessed with a vision for seafarers. While there will never be another George Charles Smith, this does not mean that maritime mission will never need someone like him. Smith was the right man at the right time, but in this he was not alone. The history of the church is punctuated by the appearance of those God uses to stir us up. Such men and women are not always at once welcomed. It is usually through the labors of authors such as Roald Kverndal that we begin to warm up to them.

Time dedicated to the understanding of "Bosun Smith" will be viewed by many as time well spent. However, the ultimate success of this work will not be judged according to its acceptance by those of us who happen to be engaged in this specific mission. The final word must rest with those mariners who remain isolated and on the margins of society, many of them, now as then, alone and without hope until another—with the faith and compassion of George Charles Smith—climbs their gangway.

David Potterton
principal chaplain, The Sailors' Society
Southampton, UK, 2011

PREFACE

A biography of George Charles Smith has been long overdue. This attempt to fill that need comes shortly after the two-hundredth anniversary of his calling to a seafarers' ministry in 1809. For Smith, as a former seafarer himself, it was especially meaningful that when the call came, it came through fellow seafarers.

For my part, the first time I heard of "Boatswain Smith," as his contemporaries called him, was in my childhood in the early 1930s. It was in the Norwegian Seamen's Church, in the docklands of Rotherhithe, London, where my family belonged to the local Norwegian seafaring community. The seafarers' pastor at the time, Reverend (later Bishop) Johannes Smidt, made sure we were all aware of the historic link between our church and that colorful character who became the founder of the worldwide Seafarers' Mission Movement.

Little could I, or my pastor, have suspected that I would one day have the privilege of researching and writing the first documented history of the beginning of the movement, *Seamen's Missions: Their Origin and Early Growth*, published in 1986. In the year 2007, I completed an updated summary of the whole movement entitled, *The Way of the Sea: The Changing Shape of Mission in the Seafaring World*. Since "Boatswain Smith" has remained the principal personality in both of these books, the present volume makes up what has become a natural maritime mission trilogy.

Throughout my research, it has continued to amaze me that no one has previously written the biography of a life so fascinating in itself and so far-reaching in its impact. Like many trailblazers before him, George

Charles Smith had his full share of eccentricities and imperfections. However, there were also fundamental features of his character that require no apology. Smith was passionate in his rejection of discrimination related to the most marginalized. This, coupled with his ceaseless solidarity with them, was of course, in complete harmony with the Savior he sought to follow. It was doubtless this sense of social justice that made "Boatswain Smith" such an instant hero for me, as a young British-born Norwegian who would later become a seafarer himself and, like Smith, eventually a seafarers' chaplain as well.

Among the more than eighty publications credited to Smith's name, none can compare, as a biographical resource, with *The Sailor's Magazine*. He would continue to edit and produce the magazine, under varying titles, from 1820 until a few days before he died—in January 1863. In his many "retrospects" in later issues, he would frequently express his wonder at the way the Lord had led him. At a particularly turbulent time, in the mid-1840s, he wrote, "The chief thing that I see ought to be done is to write my life, with all the remarkable incidents connected with it" (*The New Sailor's Magazine* 1844, p. 554). This was not to be, since it would have required a protracted leave of absence. Smith's many "distracting cares" would never have allowed for that.

In 1874, eleven years after Smith's death, it looked as though such a biography might nonetheless appear. That year, George Charles Smith's eldest son and coworker, Theophilus Smith, published an eighteen-page prospectus, entitled *The Great Moral Reformation of Sailors . . . also a Sketch of the Life and Times of the Sailors' Friend*. With a comprehensive biography in mind, he had already collected "a mass of manuscripts, correspondence, and printed works" from nearly forty years of collaboration with his father. Unfortunately, Theophilus was never able to complete his plan. In 1879, he died as a result of a railway accident.

In trying to trace the tapestry of "Boatswain Smith's" checkered life, I have set myself the goal of letting him speak for himself. The intention has been to attempt to produce a kind of autobiography based on Smith's own authorship, often from his many books, but primarily from his lifelong work—his magazine. All quotations follow the original spelling and punctuation.

Inevitably, such sources are marked by Smith's personal biases, including examples of the belligerence that characterized him throughout his life. They also reflect a choice of language typical of Smith's day, usually far more ornate than today's mode of expression. However, when used critically, these materials—especially those forty-three volumes of his own magazine—still constitute the greatest single treasure trove for any history of the early Maritime Mission Movement.

It is my hope and prayer that the result may be more than merely of historic and human interest. As the final chapter seeks to show, George Charles Smith's pioneer contributions to maritime mission are increasingly and globally relevant in this third millennium. For this, I believe, Boatswain Smith—in company with countless fellow seafarers—is greatly rejoicing. It could hardly be otherwise, as our friend follows along from his new vantage point—in the "great cloud of witnesses" we are told about in Hebrews 12:1.

Roald Kverndal
Covenant Shores, Mercer Island, Seattle, Washington
Summer 2011

ACKNOWLEDGMENTS

My personal curiosity about the amazing life story of George Charles Smith was first engendered during my childhood. I have written about this in my preface. As to Smith's adopted hometown of Penzance, I gratefully acknowledge the invaluable support I have received from many quarters.

These include especially the following: Leonard Martin Richards, a local researcher who was a direct descendant of Hannibal Curnoe, the sailor who in 1809 conveyed the call that eventually motivated Smith to devote his life to ministry among people of the sea; Reverend Hywel Roberts, pastor of a church that grew out of Smith's Jordan Chapel, the current-day Penzance Baptist Church in Clarence Street; Michael Foy, services manager of the Penwith District Council; Steve Fletcher and Frank Ruhrmund, of the newspaper *The Cornishman*; and, not least, the ever-helpful staff of the Morrab Library.

Friends in the Royal National Mission to Deep Sea Fishermen have provided me with a perfect base for my Penzance-area research visits over the years—specifically their Ship Institute in Newlyn. In that regard, my warmest thanks go to Paul Jarrett, RNMDSF mission secretary, and Reverend David Mann, their former local superintendent.

Colleagues in The Sailors' Society, the Southampton-based successor to Smith's original society of 1818, have been invaluable partners in my research from the very start. Among these, I would like to mention especially David Potterton, their current principal chaplain; Ann Brogan, operations and administration manager; Bill McCrea, senior chaplain; and Mark Warner, community relations coordinator.

I am also grateful for the fellowship and support of Richard Prendergast of Portsmouth. After captaining the mission ships *Doulos* and *Logos II,* he has since headed the Military, Naval, and Air Force Bible Society—an organization founded in 1779, well before the beginning of Smith's more comprehensive Seafarers' Mission Movement.

Smith was also instrumental in founding the Seamen's Christian Friend Society in 1846. Frank Trumble, that Society's post-World War II general secretary, gave me valuable leads in my early research. I am also thankful for continued contact with his current-day successor, Michael Wilson.

Fellow researchers in the International Association for the Study of Maritime Mission have been particularly encouraging ever since the association's origin in 1990. Especially helpful have been Dr. Stephen Friend, Dr. Alston Kennerley, Dr. Paul Mooney, and Reverend Clint Padgitt.

Research by Dr. John Lander of Truro, Cornwall, has been particularly valuable in regard to Smith's life in Penzance. Richard Blake, who facilitated my early research on Smith's 1803 visit to Reading, has provided important independent research on Smith in his academic authorship on evangelicals in the post-1775 Royal Navy. For her exceptional insights concerning Smith's mentor, John Newton, I am greatly indebted to Marylynn Rouse, coordinator of the John Newton Project.

Besides ready help by libraries elsewhere, special mention must be made of the vital professional services rendered by the British Library and the National Maritime Museum in London, the Congregational Library in Boston, Massachusetts, and the American Maritime Library at Mystic Seaport, Connecticut.

Given the specialized nature of the subject matter, it is doubtful whether this project would ever have reached port without a substantial publication and distribution fund. For this, I owe my warmest thanks to the following: Bill and Carol Matson of Kent/Seattle, US; Kirsten Kverndal of Tvedestrand, Norway; Korea International Maritime Mission of Pusan, Korea, headed by Dr. Jonah Won Jong Choi, and, most of all, the Seafarers' Trust of the International Transport Workers' Federation of

Acknowledgements

London, England, led by Tom Holmer. May they themselves be blessed by the blessing they are giving to so many others.

I deeply appreciate that William Carey Library of Pasadena, California accepted this manuscript for publication, thereby making it the third in a maritime mission trilogy. My sincere thanks go to Jeff Minard, their current general manager, Melissa Hicks as editor, and their competent colleagues. In a unique way, I am also indebted to David Shaver, the publishers' former manager. After he navigated my two previous books past so many shoals, I am so grateful he agreed to come aboard again—now in the role of content editor. Thanks, shipmate!

It would be quite impossible to list all who have supported this project in prayer over the years. Some who immediately come to mind are Karl Lauvland, Harald Daasvand, Dagfinn Kvale, Arne Johnsen, Sverre Ulvestad, Anne Arakaki-Lock, Marlowe Shoop, Steve Browne, John and Philip Vandercook, Hennie la Grange, Jim Dillenburg, Werner Strauss, Ted Maakestad, and Tom Kidd. Given our Lord's own promises about the power of prayer, the contributions of these and other faithful intercessors cannot be overestimated.

Among my many prayer partners and constant encouragers, none have surpassed my immediate family. Take grandson Jonathan, for example. For years, he has seldom met me without asking, using my Norwegian name, "How's your book doing, Bestefar?"

Last, but in a category quite her own, comes my beloved life partner Ruth. She has long believed in the need to portray the life of George Charles Smith. She has also maintained that my many years researching his life and times have left me no choice but to do my best to fill that void. It is safe to say that this book—like virtually anything worthwhile in my life—would never have come about without Ruth's gracious gifts of "faith, hope, and love."

ABBREVIATIONS

ASFS	American Seamen's Friend Society
BFBS	British and Foreign Bible Society
BFSFSBU	British and Foreign Seamen's Friend Society and Bethel Union
BFSS	British and Foreign Sailors' Society
BFSSBFU	British and Foreign Sailors' and Soldiers' Bethel Flag Union
BFSSFS	British and Foreign Seamen's and Soldiers' Friend Society
BSU	Bethel Seamen's Union
IASMM	International Association for the Study of Maritime Mission
MCS	Mariners' Church Society
MDSF	Mission to Deep Sea Fishermen (Later: Royal National Mission to Deep Sea Fishermen)
NCM	Naval Correspondence Mission
NMBS	Naval and Military Bible Society (Later: Naval, Military, and Air Force Bible Society)
PLBUS	Port of London and Bethel Union Society
PLS	Port of London Society (For Promoting Religion among Merchant Seamen)
RTS	Religious Tract Society
SCFS	Seamen's Christian Friend Society

TIMELINE
SIGNIFICANT EVENTS IN THE LIFE OF G. C. SMITH

1782   He was born on March 19 in Castle Street (now Charing Cross Road), London. His parents (both Yorkshire-born) were: William Smith, a tailor, and Nancy Wilson, daughter of a country innkeeper.

1794   As a twelve-year-old, he experienced the death of his father while living at Dover Place, Old Kent Road, on the south side of the Thames. His mother then bound him as apprentice to a major publishing business in Tooley Street.

1796   In the spring, he cast off as a fourteen-year-old cabin boy on board the American brig *Betsey*, bound for Boston via the Caribbean. Off the island of Surinam, he was forcibly enlisted by the British warship *Scipio*. Struck down by yellow fever, he was transferred to HMS *Ariadne*, repatriated, and left penniless at Sheerness.

1797   Thanks to the support of an admiral friend of his family, the fifteen-year-old shipped out as a midshipman on HMS *Agamemnon*.

1798   Disrated due to solidarity with a harshly treated fellow officer, he nevertheless advanced to the lower deck rank of "second captain of the foretop."

1801   In April, Smith served under Admiral Nelson at the Battle of Copenhagen. He narrowly escaped death while volunteering to save a sinking sister ship.

1802   After three months in Naval Hospital at Yarmouth, recovering from severe fever due to a round of self-described "wild behaviour," he was officially "invalided from the service" in March 1803, just before the Peace of Amiens.

1803   During his renewed excessive drinking with former shipmates in London, war with France broke out again. He escaped forced re-enlistment by traveling to Reading to visit a close seafarer friend.

1803   Suddenly laid low by "a virulent fever," Smith seized hold of the "small ray of hope" instilled by a Christian nurse. On March 19, he experienced, as a consequence, both his "natural and spiritual birthday."

1803   The next day, the minister and members of an adjoining chapel visited him, prayed with him, and gave him assurance of his conversion. When he was able to "crawl to the chapel," crowds of local people came to hear this "dying Nelson sailor" tell from the pulpit "what the Lord had done for his soul."

1803   In May, he left for London to bury his mother. Before she died, she had heard, to her joy, how her son had "reached his Damascus."

1803   He moved to Bath to serve as "Cellar Superintendent" for wines at York House Hotel. He also occasionally preached in local villages in cooperation with Opie Smith; a well-known Baptist lay leader in southwestern England.

1804   Smith accepted a call to ordained ministry, first voiced by Opie Smith, then formalized by the chapel to which he belonged in Reading.

1804   He commenced a three-year course of theological tuition at Plymouth Dock (now Devonport) under the local Baptist pastor, Reverend Isaiah Birt, and sponsored by Opie Smith, combining his studies with preaching around this coastal area.

1807   In October, Smith was called and installed to fill a vacancy at the Baptists' "Octagon chapel" in the port city of Penzance. His preaching soon led to an extension of the chapel, which he now renamed "Jordan Chapel."

1808   He married Theodosia Skipworth, daughter of Baptist parents in Yorkshire. During the next few years in Penzance, she gave birth to ten children.

1809   Smith was invited by some seafarers to preach on board their revenue cutter, the *Dolphin*, which had just survived a harrowing storm. He would later come to see this as his new "life calling"—a ministry dedicated to people of the sea.

1809   News from the *Dolphin* about Bible study groups on Royal Navy ships in the Napoleonic War prompted Smith to write encouraging letters to sailors who could alert him about other "religious" crew on board.

1809   Smith developed a network of pastoral counseling by mail, which he called a "Naval Correspondence Mission"—his first maritime ministry enterprise.

1811   Based on incidents from this "Naval Awakening," as well as experiences from his own years at sea, Smith started a seven-part series of popular sailor dialogues called *The Boatswain's Mate*.

1812   Smith preached in several major London chapels and launched the first-ever public campaign to promote the welfare of seafarers—the "Sailors' Cause."

1814   Although it meant digressing from his primary call, Smith took time this year to offer chaplaincy to soldiers in Wellington's Peninsular Army in France and Spain, as well as to sailors in a few port cities there. Then, from 1815 to 1818, he went on to provide food, work, and spiritual nurture to the isolated inhabitants of the Scilly Islands in the English Channel.

1817   Smith discovered how Bible study groups on North Country collier ships were meeting on the Thames under an emblem of their own, the "Bethel Flag." He eagerly joined in himself and preached to huge crowds from ship and shore.

1817   Smith envisaged converting a ship into a floating chapel, enlisted the support of a London shipbroker and supplied him with a tract called *The British Ark . . . an Attempt to Obtain a Floating Place of Worship*.

1818 Smith helped secure a 379-ton former sloop of war, the *Speedy*. On March 18, 1818, he facilitated the founding of the Port of London Society (BFSSFS) for Promoting Religion among Merchant Seamen (PLS)—a worldwide first.

1819 Seeing the need for a further society that could promote the outreach of the Bethel Flag, Smith founded the Bethel Union on November 12, 1819. It was later called the British and Foreign Seamen's Friend Society and Bethel Union.

1825 Convinced of the necessity for a second maritime sanctuary in London, Smith formed a Mariners' Church Society, leasing for that purpose the former Danish-Norwegian Church in Wellclose Square. The following year, he moved from Penzance to this hub of London's "Sailortown."

1827 Smith founded the first-ever "Destitute Sailors' Asylum" in nearby Dock Street—the first step in his attempt to transform Wellclose Square from a "Sailors' Sodom and Gomorrah" to a "New Marine Jerusalem." This Asylum constituted a clear counterattack against crew exploitation by the widespread "Crimping System."

1828 Smith seized upon the collapse of the notorious Brunswick Theatre in adjacent Well Street to raise the world's first "Sailors' Home" on the ruined site. Finally completed in 1835, the building was planned to provide safe facilities for discharged (as opposed to destitute) sailors ashore. Soon emulated both in Britain and abroad.

1829 Smith was exposed to a harsh published attack entitled *An Appeal to the Public* by a new secretary/editor of the Port of London and Bethel Union Society (PLBUS), an 1827 merger of both of Smith's former societies. Leaders from each of these at once wrote a counterpublication called *Refutation*, justifying Smith's initiative in founding the Mariners' Church Society (MCS).

Timeline: Significant Events in the Life of G. C. Smith

1832 A public reconciliation was attempted between the MCS, now renamed the British and Foreign Seamen's and Soldiers' Friend Society (BFSFS), and the PLBUS. In October, when these efforts broke down, Smith founded the British and Foreign Sailors' and Soldiers' Bethel Flag Union (BFSSBFU).

1833 In July, the PLBUS merged into a new society called the British and Foreign Sailors' Society (BFSS). This has since grown into the major twenty-first century Southampton-based Sailors' Society.

1836 Despite a series of important welfare initiatives, Smith became embroiled in libelous attacks on both him and his society, culminating in the first of four terms in debtors' prisons.

1845 Smith's fourth arrest resulted from his inability to pay the rent on the Mariners' Church. Despite losing his church, Smith still hung on to his other vital asset, *The Sailor's Magazine*. (After launching it in 1820, he continued editing the magazine under varying titles until the year he died.)

1848 After having helped two years earlier to found the Seamen's Christian Friend Society, Smith accepted a call to return to Penzance and take up his former pastorate there.

1853 Smith resigned his pastorate in order to continue traveling, ministering, and writing in the *Seamen's Cause*.

1861 He received an invitation to visit seafarers' centers along the East Coast of the US. Here he was feted as the founder of the worldwide missionary movement among seafarers.

1863 On January 10, Smith passed away peacefully in his sleep, almost eighty-one years of age. His funeral in Penzance Cemetery on January 16 was attended by an estimated 2,000 people, including several clergy of different denominations.

CHAPTER 1
EARLY YEARS
(1782–1796)

Looking back at the beginning of his life, George Charles Smith wrote in his later years, "My father, William Smith, was a plain man, a native of the city of York and a tailor by trade. As a young man, he moved to the city of Knottingly, near Ferry Bridge in Yorkshire. Here, at that time, my dear mother, Nancy Wilson, lived in her native place, where her father kept a country inn. It was also here that my father became acquainted with my mother and married her."

"Sometime after their marriage," Smith continued, "I have understood, they removed to the town of Pontefract, also in Yorkshire, where they kept a small public house. Around 1772, they moved to London and settled there. My father became converted, as I have been told, at George Whitefield's Tottenham Court Road Chapel, not far distant. Later, he became a member of Surrey Chapel in Blackfriars Road."

William Smith's wife also "became the subject of divine grace," and was subsequently made "chapel-keeper of Lady Huntingdon's Chapel in Westminster, near Tothill Street." This was thanks to "the influence of the pious governor of Tothills Fields Prison, George Smith." Named after this family benefactor, George Charles Smith was born on March 19, 1782, while his family was living in Castle Street—since then renamed Charing Cross Road, near Leicester Square. At that time, according to Smith, his parents were "neither elevated by rank, nor distinguished by wealth, but struggling through life with a numerous and a very disobedient and trying family."

Not long afterwards, Smith's ailing, asthmatic father found he needed to move to other living quarters on the south side of the Thames—Dover Place, Old Kent Road, then considered "a sort of country place." Here, during Smith's early childhood, he was often left in the care of his father who tried as best he could to carry on his vocation as a tailor. William Smith enrolled his son in a Sunday school at nearby Surrey Chapel, Blackfriars Road. Here the small boy reportedly displayed such an "ardor" that it attracted the attention of the chapel's Congregational minister, Reverend Rowland Hill, renowned in his day as one of the nation's most prominent preachers.

Meanwhile, Smith's more robust mother had been maintaining "a respectable lodging-house in Castle Street," and at one point also kept "a pork shop in York Street, Westminster." Eventually, the whole family settled in Boundary Row by Blackfriars Road, on the south side of the River Thames. Here, from the age of seven, Smith attended Bermondsey Parish School at Bermondsey Church. In 1794, at the age of twelve, he experienced the tragedy of the death of his frail father. His mother later remarried, this time to an organ builder and Baptist deacon, Mr. Hayman. She continued living in Boundary Row until she herself passed away in 1803.

When Smith's father died, his mother "bound" her twelve-year-old son as apprentice to a large bookselling and publishing concern in Tooley Street, Southwark, "near Chamberlain's Wharf by London Bridge." For the next two years, the lad had "daily intercourse with Paternoster Row," the hub of the metropolitan publishing world. This position opened the opportunity to satisfy the youngster's thirst for knowledge. Day or night, sometimes till three in the morning, he read histories, popular works, all he could come by. Looking back in later years on his prolific authorship, Smith would have good reason to reflect, "Here I was literally trained up for all my present work."

In starting her son George on a land-based career, Nancy Smith presumably lived in the hope that he would not follow the example of his two elder brothers and go to sea. If so, her fears were understandable. Young George had already visited with William when this brother arrived on the Thames as chief mate of a "West Indiaman." George had listened with rapt interest to his tales of exotic lands. William would later become "chief mate or captain of a large American ship from Philadelphia, where he had a wife and family." He was feared to have lost his life at sea, possibly linked to his heavy drinking. George also discovered that Thomas, his other brother, had "perished in a distant land, after losing both his legs in a desperate battle at sea," while in the naval service off Trincomalee, in the East Indies.

It is not entirely unthinkable that the family's strong Yorkshire roots may, perhaps subconsciously, have influenced all three brothers' attraction toward a seafaring life. After all, York—formerly called "Jorvik"—was once the capital of the seafaring Norsemen who settled in those parts. The seaports of Yorkshire continued the rich maritime heritage of the North Country coast, recently reaffirmed by the epic voyages of one of England's greatest navigators, Yorkshire-born Captain James Cook.

Both within and around the Thames-side workplace of young George, he inevitably came into close contact with many captains and mates, as well as "hosts of sailors." Here he continued for two years until the call of the sea became too strong. In his undated book entitled *The Log-Book: A Review of Various Circumstances in the Voyage of Life that Contributed to Originate the Present Important Diffusion of Religion in the Maritime World*, Smith has detailed the fascinating narrative of how he managed to overcome his mother's pleadings and finally put to sea:

> Having quitted the situation I had lived in, I visited a brig in which a school-fellow had shipped, and, in company with others, ascended to the masthead, in a frolic on the Sabbath afternoon. Being accustomed in sport to climb the highest trees in the vicinity of London, I determined to ascend by the futtock-shrouds [in the rigging], and go up higher than any one else. The Mate of the ship observed me from the deck, and on my coming down, said, "Well done, my lad, you have beat to windward of all the rest, you'd make a first-rate sailor; I'd have you dock your coat, and bend a new pair of trowsers, and ship for the East or West Indies; and after weathering a few gales, I think you'll make a smart fellow to hand, reef or steer."

This compliment to my agility decided me at once for a sailor's life, and no remonstrance of my mother or friends could shake my resolution. I took several opportunities of going on board different ships. Finding out I could not get a berth, I went round to all the coffee-houses about Cornhill frequented by masters of ships; and, wherever I found a group of this description, addressed them, "Captain, do you want a boy to go to sea with you?" Many jeered, some swore, some asked me the most indecent questions, while others told me to "be off."

I persevered for several days, until a captain, sitting alone in a box, seeing me rejected with many coarse jokes of some reprobate captains, he called as I was leaving the coffee-house, "Hello, here, my lad, about ship." I turned round, and walked to him, when he looked at me very mildly and said, "Well, my fine fellow, and what do you want?" "A ship, Sir." "Was you ever at sea?" "No, Sir." "Then what makes you wish to go now?" "Because I like it, Sir; I'd rather be a sailor than a king." "A gale of wind would shake your confidence, my boy." "Never mind that; will you hire me, Sir, in your ship? I'm all ready." "Where do you wish to go?" "Any where; don't care where it is. I'll go with you all over the world if you like."

"But I'm an American, and if you ship with me, I should like you to become a citizen of America, which could be easily done when we arrive there." "O I don't mind that; you may make me a Dutchman if you like; only let me go to sea with you." "I am pleased with your manner, and if you can bring your mother next Monday to my lodging on Tower Hill, I shall have no objection, if agreeable to her to have you bound an apprentice to me for seven years." "Thank you, Sir, depend on it. I'll be there, and mother too."

On the following Monday we waited on the captain, who received us with great kindness. My dear mother said, "Allow me, Sir, to ask for your place of residence in America." "My name, Madam, is Clark, the brig I command is called the *Betsey*, we belong to Salem, near Boston, where my family are at present." "Well, Sir, my dear boy has brought me here to bind him apprentice; he knows my disinclination to his views, but as he will not settle to any trade, and is determined for the sea, I must reluctantly comply with his wishes. I have, however, confidence in my George, he has been brought up at a Sunday school, he reads a great deal, he has been a good boy to me; and with an intelligent mind, I should hope in time he will possess the grace of God, and become useful in the world."

"You speak very properly, Madame, about your son, and it will, perhaps, give you some satisfaction to know, that I always attend Divine worship with my family, when I am at home, and so does my mate." "I had many fears about my son, and dreaded that he would fall into the hands of some swearing reprobate man; but when I heard you was an *American,* I was pleased, for I have heard an excellent account of America, and I know the gospel is faithfully preached there; you must have many persons there, Sir, who love the Lord Jesus Christ, and without *love to him,* what is a country, what is the world, and what is life itself?" "True, Madam, but America is like other places, we have many bad persons, and many good ones. Religion prevails much in some places. The Almighty will certainly take care of your son."

The business was soon settled and the captain gave me permission to see my friends, get some suitable clothes ready, and then ordered me to join the brig at *Cherry Garden Stairs.* The captain intended that I should take the situation as cabin boy, and in the mean time a black boy procured from the West Indies was to instruct me. The first Sabbath I had "bent my first rigging," as the sailors term it, I appeared in the gallery of Surrey Chapel, in jacket and trowsers. Many of my schoolfellows congratulated me at the close of the service, that I was going on so fine a voyage."

Following farewell with his concerned mother—"in a way that might be expected"—the fourteen-year-old cabin boy cast off in the spring of 1796, bound for Boston via the Dutch colony of Surinam in the Caribbean. During the voyage, Captain Clark, whom Smith describes in warm terms as a father figure, gave him "the most solemn assurances" of making him mate the last two years of his apprenticeship. He would then, if he studied navigation well and conducted himself "with propriety," get him the command of an American ship. As it transpired, the *Betsey*'s port of call in the Caribbean changed all that. In his reminiscences, Smith has recounted the drama that ensued:

> The morning was exceedingly fine when we arrived off the [Dutch] island of Surinam, which had recently been blockaded by the British. We were surprised to find an English line of battleship, the *Scipio,* sixty-four guns, still at anchor off the harbour. We hoisted the colours of the United States, thinking they would protect us, but a few shots across our bows convinced us that we must run up and speak their Guard Ship. A six-oared cutter, well armed, soon pulled towards us, and ordered the anchor to be let go and the sails furled within a convenient range of shot, in case we attempted to escape.

> My shipmate and I determined we would let the English see what we could do; I had by this time become so much of an American, that I already talked of the English as of foreigners. We were unusually smart in rolling up the top-gallant sails and to show how adventurous we could be, chasing each other from rope to rope.

> All this cost me dear enough. I afterwards understood, that the Captain of the *Scipio* walking the quarter deck observed me, and on asking our Captain what boy that was, he said he was an English lad he had brought from London. The Captain of the *Scipio* immediately said, "I'll have him then." Captain Clark tried all he could, assuring him that I was his apprentice, and he understood that no man-of-war could impress an apprentice out of a merchant ship. The Captain of the *Scipio* had, however, formed his determination, and was not to be shaken. I laughed to our Mate and said, "I am legally bound apprentice to Captain Clark." "True," said he, "but you are not in the River Thames, you are in the West Indies, and you'll find very little law or Gospel here." With a sorrowful heart I went down below, and rolled my clothes up, and handed them upon deck, where I went to take leave; they were all much affected at the separation.

> As the officer of the boat cried "Shove off" I cannot describe the terror of mind that filled me at this moment. I was ignorant of a man-of-war, but the idea I had formed of it, connected with the

unjust manner in which I was torn from our little crew, and the language I had heard, intermixed with most horrid oaths, both from the officer and the boat's crew, had contributed to fill me with horror so strong that I really believe nothing but a religious education kept me from jumping overboard, and trying to drown myself. It was a moon-light night, and as we approached the ship, my fears were not at all decreased, when I saw her immense size, compared with the *Betsey* brig. The rows of cannon presented to my view such a warlike appearance that it really alarmed me.

Captain Clark, remembering his promise to young George's mother back in London, even managed to visit the *Scipio*'s captain in his cabin in order to show him the boy's indenture papers, but to no avail. After a tearful farewell, Smith's life would thereafter take a very different turn, with long-term consequences no one could have imagined. All of which resulted from the captain of a British man-of-war finding himself short of crew and therefore resorting to the standard system of condoned kidnapping known as "impressment."

As such, this practice was seen as an effective means of securing sufficient recruits for the island nation's navy (her "wooden walls") in time of war or national emergency. This form of naval enslavement had already come under heavy fire from activists in the Slave Trade Abolition Movement, such as Britain's William Wilberforce. When broadened to include the merchant ships of a supposedly sovereign nation—as in the case of the Boston-registered *Betsey*—the policy became so deeply resented that it eventually became a major cause of America's War of 1812 against her former colonial overlords.

In his autobiographical publication, *The Log-Book*, Smith gives graphic detail of the traumatic effect of the practice of impressment on a London lad, not yet fifteen years of age. On His Majesty's ship *Scipio*, Smith was abruptly introduced to the brutal realities of daily life in the British wartime navy. As it turned out, his stay on the *Scipio* was cut short due to the deadly disease to which so many Europeans would fall victim in the tropics. Together with numerous others on board, he was struck down by a violent attack of yellow fever. While at Martinico, he saw many of his shipmates die an agonizing death as a result. For his part, Smith some-how survived. However, he was by then so debilitated that he had to be drafted to a convoy escort, HMS *Ariadne*, for repatriation.

After being battered by a series of winter storms, the *Ariadne* ar-rived at the British naval base of Spithead near Portsmouth. Here, the impressionable young boy was confronted by the level of temptations to which newly arrived sailors were traditionally exposed. Smith would later make this practice a subject of constant campaigning. In one retrospect, he recounts how, as soon as his vessel had cast anchor, "boat loads of sea harlots, with bladders of strong drink concealed about their persons, were scattered all around the ship, so that for a week or ten days His Majesty's ship *Ariadne* became the greatest floating hell in the world."

When the ship reached her final destination at the port of Sheerness on the Thames, Smith went through another harrowing experience. This, too, would one day be put to good purpose. Duly discharged with the rest of the ship's company, the young boy found himself simply "left upon the beach there to perish," as he put it. Without any clothes but what he had on, and without the money to pay his fare home, he learned what it meant to be "a forlorn destitute sea boy." Somehow, he struggled back to Bound-ary Row—and a very anxious mother—just before Christmas of 1796.

CHAPTER 2
A FLOATING HELL
(1797-1802)

After all young George had been through during the prior months, it would have been understandable if any craving for a seafaring career had been snuffed out. In Smith's case, however, the call of the sea ran deep and once more proved irresistible. But this time better provision was made before casting off. The family's pastor, Reverend Rowland Hill, a relative of Admiral John Holloway, was enlisted for the purpose. To exercise influence through "family interest" on behalf of a promising youth was at that time nothing unusual. In fact, this was altogether in keeping with long-standing officer recruitment tradition in the Royal Navy.

So it was as Admiralty midshipman that young Smith, now fifteen years old, traveled back to Sheerness in March 1797. Here he joined His Majesty's ship-of-the-line, *Agamemnon* of sixty-four guns. This had been Horatio Nelson's vessel during the first three years of the Revolutionary War with France (1793–1802). It was now the vessel on which Smith would serve "during the heat of war" for his remaining five years in the Royal Navy.

However, Smith's service in an officer's rank aboard the *Agamemnon* would not be without complications. Grateful as he was for his childhood pastor at Surrey Chapel, Midshipman Smith soon had to deal with derision by his peers. "When I first went to sea," he later reminisced, "the sailors called me 'Rowland Hill,' because I spoke much about his church and Sunday school, where I had been brought up." In May of the same year, during the notorious naval mutiny at the Nore led by Richard Parker, Smith found himself confined to his cabin like the rest of the quarterdeck. Here he was "at the mercy of a crew of 500 men, who seized the ship, and joined a squadron of mutineers."

There was more to come. In the course of the following year, the young midshipman fell into disfavor with his commander. Apparently, he had signed a petition in favor of an officer messmate whom the captain was "determined to have tried by a court-martial." As a result, the now sixteen-year-old Smith was demoted from his rank as midshipman during the vessel's stay at Hull in 1798.

Although Smith himself would later describe this decision as "cruel," it did not prevent him from making the most of his misfortune, eventually advancing to become a "second captain of the foretop." This was decidedly a "lower-deck" position, but it was especially exposed and called for a high level of courage and skill. In fact, just as Smith's first feat of seamanship as a child was to climb the mast of a ship without permission, he could now boast about how—among his peers—he became "the first to mount aloft, and run out to the yard-arm to reef top-sails."

While serving aboard the *Agamemnon* from 1797 to 1802, "in storms and battles, and hells afloat and ashore," Smith would survive two major naval engagements. The first, while still a midshipman, was under Admiral Adam Duncan, defeating the Dutch at the Battle of Camperdown in October 1797. The second was when serving in the foretop under Admiral Horatio Nelson, engaging the Danes at the Battle of Copenhagen in April 1801.

Smith would frequently revert to the latter critical event in many of his reminiscences. Here follows a compendium offering rare insights into the psychology of seafarers before, during, and after a major action in the days of sail. It is made up entirely of excerpts from various issues of Smith's magazine between 1852 and 1859, as well as from autobiographical parts of the most popular of his books, *The Boatswain's Mate*:

> The year 1801 was one of the most perilous years for England. Our fleets were demanded, winter and summer, to blockade the Dutch fleet in Holland, the Spanish fleet at Cadiz, and the French fleets at Brest and Toulon. But now, by some influence from France, it appeared that Paul, the Emperor of Russia, had laid an embargo

on our English ships in Russian ports, and also prevailed upon the Baltic nations of Denmark and Sweden to form a *Northern Confederacy* against England.

Early in the year 1801 it was generally expected that war by the Northern Powers would be declared against England, and when the ice broke in the Baltic, about March, that the combined fleets of Russia, Denmark and Sweden would sail from the Baltic and invade England. It was considered, to prevent [such an] invasion, an immense fleet should be collected, [even though] it was most dangerous to send such a fleet through the storms of the North Sea at this time. Admiral Nelson, [now] so celebrated [after] St. Vincent and the Nile, was commanded to join Admiral Sir Hyde Parker in command.

But alas! At this time, England cared nothing about the souls of her sailors. The country provided ships and wages for them at sea, and dens of vice for them on shore. But as to their immortal souls and eternity, they were supposed to be a people so unfit for heaven, that it would be idle and useless to direct them there. . . .

We sailed from Yarmouth Roads March 12th, 1801. We suffered most dreadfully for nearly a week in the North Sea. One of our fleet, the *Invincible*, 74, was lost. At length we reached the Scaw Point anchorage. [Meanwhile] Mr. Vansittart from the English Government [went] up to Elsineur [to negotiate] permission to pass the Sound Channel, and sail up to Russia with all the fleet of war.

This was refused, and our admirals [decided] that we now force the passage. The first shot fired at our fleet would be considered a declaration of war by the Northern Confederacy. The Sound was protected on the Swedish side at our left hand by the fort of Helsingborg, and on that of Denmark by the Castle of Cronenberg [at Elsineur]. It had long been considered impossible to force a passage through the Sound.

No man not in a fleet can imagine the horrors of conscience and the emotions in such long delayed anticipations of war and bloodshed, and [yet] no religious preparation for it. Our battles generally had been a sudden rush into action. But here all was deliberate and on the mind for days. O, what pale, agitated countenances I saw among the crowd of men on our forecastle among the greatest drunkards, blasphemers, and whoremongers. Not a man but trembled, all ready for battle—yet not one soul ready for eternity! I was like the rest, only, having been a Sunday school boy at Surrey Chapel, and with a pious father and mother in London, I knew more about sin and hell. So, officers' cry for *"King and Country"* could not quell the risings of conscience and the prospects of death and judgment.

Early on March 31st, the signal was made by Lord Nelson to "Prepare for Action." Nelson led the van, steering close to the Swedish coast, risking all the shot firing from Helsingborg. We expected this to be very great, but not equal to the firing from Elsineur. We had heard much of the artillery at Elsineur. We [in the *Agamemnon*] were about the fourth ship in line following him [Nelson]. I was one of the most daring, desperate men on board, doing duty as second captain of the foretop. I determined to run up the shrouds of our fore-rigging and narrowly watch Nelson the moment he was fired at from Elsineur, to see if he engaged Helsingborg as well, because then we would [be] cut to pieces, as we were so near the Swedish shore.

The moment Nelson's ship arrived on a line with Cronenberg Castle, they opened the most tremendous fire. I saw the first broadside from Nelson's ship to return this fire. [But] the smoke deceived me, and I ran down the rigging, jumped on the forecastle, and cried out aloud, "Clear away the guns! Nelson is engaged on both sides. We shall have hot work, if we live...." I have never been able to remember anything more. All were at work with the guns, crying out amidst the roar of cannon, "Hold on," "Get ready," "England for ever," "Cheer up," "Goodbye, shipmate," "My turn next," "Fight for King and Country," "A good drop of grog when we are done," [and more of] such idle nonsense.

The shot at our right hand fell like showers of hail near us. But not one shot was fired upon us from the Swedish coast. We were all perfectly astonished at this amazing forbearance on the part of

Sweden. Having forced the Sound, [we] anchored at the entrance of the Baltic Sea, with Copenhagen in sight [and ranged against us] all the fleet of block ships, ships-of-the-line and sea coast batteries. [So once again] we had a long time of gloomy anticipation....

The Battle of Copenhagen 1801, during which Smith served on HMS Agamemnon *under Admiral Nelson. (Eidem and Lutken, History of Our Naval Power)*

My most intimate friend, John Lovegrove [and I] took our pipes to smoke and talk about the morrow, while most of the men were down below at their dinner and grog. I said, "What do you think about to-morrow, John?" He shook his head and cried, "The last day for many of us...." We now could not avoid shedding a tear about home, and he said, "I have aft a letter in my chest. If I should be killed, send it to my aunt at Reading, if you live." I said, "I have also left a letter. Send it to my mother if I am killed tomorrow."

We could not stand this. He fled to a corner, and I looked round, longing for some place where I could kneel and try to pray, as my father and mother [used to do]. But I was afraid and ashamed to be seen on my knees, as every man would have ridiculed me, and called out *Methodist*—which at that time was a most contempt-ible word, and meant *coward*. But looking up to our large foretop, I hastened aloft, where no man might see me. I kneeled down before the head of my foremast, and in my ignorance as an unconverted man, said, "O God, please let me not be killed in battle to-morrow. But please let me live and go home to see mother—and I'll never do anything bad again as long as I live."

With that ignorance, I hastened down on deck, all ready to fight now; because we were told it was all right fighting for king and country, and God was merciful to sailors....Such was the state of thousands in our fleet. Not one man knew any better—sent out to fight by Christian England! Shame, shame on our country, thus to neglect us! With no Bible or minister to warn us from the wrath to come, by a just and righteous God. We never had a chaplain since 1797, and [even] then it was only reading and prayers, and telling us to be good . . . .

Friday, April 2nd 1801, O what a gloomy, melancholy morning, as this was the day of battle, and Nelson was to lead us on to blood and slaughter. Only, perhaps, we [might] not be killed, but conquer and take prizes. This was all the heaven we looked for; and Nelson was considered our Saviour and our God. Dreadful sentiment— about going to Heaven for fighting—invented by devils and propagated by madmen! Can the fire of an enemy introduce a soul into Heaven? Or a mere act of duty to the country atone for the sins of an abandoned life? Then, indeed, had Christ died in vain . . . .

But now nine a.m. had passed, and as our ship was to be the second ship in the line, we who belonged to the tops hastened aloft. We had just made sail when, to our astonishment, we could not weather a shoal or quicksand, and stuck fast. HMS *Russell*, 74, and HMS *Bellona*, 74, followed our ship [and all three] were grounded so fast that they remained here during all the battle.

[Besides those] three line-of-battle ships which had struck upon shoals of sand in Copenhagen Roads, few ships of the fleet were more damaged by the showers of shot from ships and batteries than HMS *Ardent*, 64. To relieve the *Ardent*, an officer on the quarter deck of the *Agamemnon* cried aloud, "Fifty men must be sent on board the *Ardent*, to repair damages, help the wounded, and supply the place of the killed there. Who will volunteer?" I rushed aft, as belonging to the foretop and well acquainted with rigging, and exclaimed, "I volunteer for the *Ardent!*" Boats were ordered up and we were rowed on board. We hastened down to the after cockpit, shoveled up heaps of congealed blood to clear the deck and render aid to the many who had arms or legs shot off and were dying.

[During the action that followed], some shot struck the loose part of my jacket; others just passed over my head. Some whizzed by my cheek and almost burnt me with the wind; others struck the place where I had been standing the moment before, and threw up a thousand splinters. A gun burst next to ours and killed fifteen men; four guns at which I served successively were cleared of every man but myself. Oh, the goodness of God, to [spare] a wretch like me! Oh, that brothers of English and Danes should thus have been forced to murder each other for the ambition of one man in Paris and the madness of another in St. Petersburg.

When Nelson saw three ships aground, and that Admiral Parker could not get up sufficiently, and when he anticipated the desperate havoc the Danes might produce at night by bombshell and fire-ships, he wrote a letter "To the brothers of Englishmen—the Danes," addressed to the Crown Prince of Denmark, requesting a truce of twelve hours. It was the most unaccountably humane act that the Danish government agreed to a truce; for had they continued to fire from the batteries that night, our ships would have been cut to pieces, and scarcely an officer or man left alive.

With the French flotillas that were ready for invasion at Boulogne, had a righteous God permitted the Danes to have refused a truce, England might have beheld her palaces, churches, chapels, mansions, and shops in flames, amidst the ruthless plunder and devastation from French and Spanish forces. It was not Nelson, but God, who saved the country from all these horrors. In gratitude to the Danes, we ought ever to remember this most extraordinary act of national kindness and humanity.

Smith expressed similar sentiments also for the Swedes who, instead of descending from their nearby naval base of Carlscrona upon the battered British fleet at Copenhagen, held back and entered upon an armistice. Finally, Smith also describes how peace proposals were received from Russia too, on Alexander's timely accession to the imperial throne. Thus, according to Smith, was removed the ominous threat of the Northern Powers in the spring of 1801. Thus, too, was the future Founder of Seafarers' Missions able to continue a form of education in the "University of the Sea" that would one day prove invaluable.

Despite his deliverance during the Battle of Copenhagen, Smith commented, "Whenever I landed afterwards, whether in Denmark, Prussia or Russia, I pursued my old course of sin, without the least remorse." After returning from the Baltic later in 1801, the *Agamemnon* carried on "knocking about a great part of the winter in the North Sea." Finally, Smith records that they anchored in Yarmouth Roads, in order to spend some weeks there.

In Yarmouth, after a new round of wild behavior, Smith contracted a bout of fever so acute that it landed him in the ship's sick bay. "Reduced at length to a mere skeleton," he states, he was "ordered on shore, and dragged up in a cart from the beach to the Naval Hospital." There he continued to lie for weeks—in a stupor so alarming his physicians did not expect him to survive. After three months, "to the astonishment of all around," he did eventually recover and was able to leave Yarmouth and the navy, officially certified as "invalided from the service." This was just a few weeks before the short-lived Peace of Amiens, 1802–1803.

By the beginning of 1802, Britain and France were both near exhaustion through the mutual toll of nine years of continuous war. In March of that year, both nations welcomed the breathing space provided at Amiens.

For Napoleon, it gave him an opportunity to free France from distractions in the Western Hemisphere. Faced with the reality of British naval superiority in the Atlantic, he managed to sell his country's vast Louisiana Territory to the US by May 1803. By then he had also given up the French colony of Haiti, after losing out to the island's liberator, Toussain l'Ouverture, the self-educated slave who had become beloved by his people as a "Black Napoleon."

For the British, initial war-weary relief dissipated quickly, as both sides accused the other of noncompliance with the peace terms. Meanwhile, the British saw reasons to fear that Napoleon was rebuilding his fleet in preparation for the invasion of Britain. In self-interest, Britain therefore declared war against France again in May 1803.

CHAPTER 3
BOUND FOR "DAMASCUS"
(1802-1803)

As soon as Smith was free to leave Yarmouth Naval Hospital in early 1802, he set forth to rejoin his mother in London—and did so in style. He made sure to obtain a "hackney coach" to carry him home the last stretch. As for his mother, having understood that her son was dying, her fears overcame her when he arrived, and she fell "insensible to the earth." Smith relates how he "bathed her cheeks, crying 'Mother! O, my dear mother!'" He then promised her to "depart from sin and serve the Lord." After all, now he was "free from a man-of-war" and could anticipate "many opportunities of hearing the Gospel and attending to her pious advice."

True enough, he did start to attend church regularly, together with his mother, both at Surrey Chapel and elsewhere. Also, he found a job: "A situation of respectability offered at a wine and brandy merchant, on St. Mary's Hill." However, he knew all too well that "a good smart spell in the Sick Bay" could not in itself teach him how to "steer" his life, when once he was taken off "the doctor's list." It was simply "not in the power of pain to change the heart and renew the life." That, he realized, could only happen through Christ's "all-sufficient grace working by these means."

In addition, Smith met his discharged shipmates in London. With them, he returned "like the dog to his vomit" (Prov 26:11). Urged by Smith's ignoble example, his buddies all "gloried in hailing their leader." It built up to what happened one Saturday night at the Royal Circus in Blackfriars Road (later known as the New Surrey Theatre). This is Smith's version, as reproduced in Part II of *The Boatswain's Mate*:

Being on shore in London with several shipmates, after rolling about the streets and drinking excessively, we rushed into the Royal Circus in Blackfriars Road, and entered the gallery while the actors were performing. The house was crowded. I proposed that we should fight our way with the sticks we had to the front of the gallery, and each of us leap from thence into the pit. This was resolved on, with dreadful imprecations on any man that failed.

I sallied forth, leading the van and desperately encountering everyone that opposed us. After many struggles with the audience, I reached the front of the gallery, and sang out to the people below, "Stand from under there!" Several gentlemen interposed to prevent me. But I fought with a large stick like a madman. Calling to my shipmates, "Are you all ready? Here goes!" I leaped off—a gentleman caught me by the greatcoat, and hung me there until others could drag me in.

Smith as ringleader in a Sailortown spree, 1802.
(The Boatswain's Mate, Part II)

The theatre was all confusion—the acting was stopped—and the runners dragged my shipmates downstairs in the most brutal manner. A police officer seized me—a scuffle ensued—I struck him with such violence as to endanger his life. I endeavored to escape; but a blow from another officer across my arm rendered it useless, and they overpowered me. I attempted to raise a mob to rescue me. But the officer forced us into a coach, and hurried us into St. George's Watch-house, in the Borough. There we roared and sang the most infamous songs until three o'clock on the Sabbath morning, when we fell asleep.

At seven o'clock, we were roused by the people in the street calling to us, and identifying us as poor harmless sailors, who only happened to be drunk. We told a piteous tale, and they bought us liquor until we were almost intoxicated again. I strove to be merry, but my conscience struck me to that degree, that I shook with horror at my situation. My companions knew nothing and cared for nothing. But I had received a religious education. Besides, whenever I was on shore, respect for my aged mother induced me to be externally decent before her; and particularly to observe the Sabbath Day with her in the house of God. It was now eleven o'clock on Sabbath morning. My mother would have been at the house of God—but for me!

About one o'clock, information arrived that my dearest mother was at an adjoining public-house, where the officers had conducted her; that she had obtained bail for our appearances at Union Hall, and was waiting for me. I thought I could have met a thousand cannons' mouths with ease, compared to what I felt at encountering the tender expostulations of such a mother....She drew me gently to her, reclining her head upon my shoulders, and with heavy sobs exclaimed, "My child yet lives! O God, I thank Thee!"

Smith had been aware that his mother, in the latter part of her life, was "much afflicted with a cancer in her breast." As he put it, "Never did I witness such acute agonies, or such pious resignation as in her case. I admired religion for the supports it yielded. But being yet unregenerate, I could only admire and continue as a stranger to its inward joys . . . Now conscience would harrow up my soul with the thought that my conduct would speedily murder my venerable parent."

That March in 1803, it had become obvious that the precarious Peace of Amiens was fast crumbling. A "hot press" for sailors was the inevitable result. Smith was advised to take to the country for a fortnight until the press gang had "cooled." He made a swift decision to leave London for Oxford. On the way, he decided to honor the invitation of his special shipmate from the *Agamemnon*, John Lovegrove, and spend a few days with him in his hometown of Reading in Berkshire. It was here that Smith was finally "stopped in his mad career"—an outcome he would later compare with what happened to Saul of Tarsus on his way to Damascus, as depicted in Acts 9.

On his arrival in Reading, Smith had only just registered at the "Jack of Newbury" public house in Horn Street, when he suddenly became severely ill with a virulent fever. He lay "for three long days, in the greatest horror of mind and danger, expecting to die and perish in his sins." Dr. Golding, of nearby London Street, advised Lovegrove to have his friend removed to "a plain cottage in a court at London Street where a nurse to the sick resided."

Here, Smith was carried carefully in a sedan chair, passing through a graveyard en route and arriving in the morning of March 19. "Afraid to die, yet indifferent to life," Smith somehow seized upon "a small ray of hope" given by his new nurse. She had simply reminded him, "He does not despise prayer, Sir. The Lord can save your soul!" In later life, Smith would constantly refer to March 19, 1803—which was also his date of birth—as both his "natural and spiritual birthday." He saw it as the day when his spiritual life took off in a completely different direction.

On the next morning, Sunday March 20, at seven o'clock, he heard—to his great surprise—persons singing the hymn he knew as a Sunday school boy, to the tune his mother and sisters so often sang at his home in Boundary Row: "Jesus sought me when a stranger, wandering from the field of God, he, to save my soul from danger, interposed his precious blood." That morning, Smith was, by his own account, "persuaded by the nurse to write a note to the minister, as a poor dying sailor from Nelson's fleet, asking him to pray for him and for his poor sick mother in London also." The minister, Mr. Weller, surprised at such a note, prayed earnestly and read the note to the people.

> On the evening of this Sabbath day, the afflicted and trembling sailor was carefully lifted out of his bed and carried to an arm chair, and placed near the wall which divided the chapel from the sick room. Here he heard the minister preach from some verse in Jeremiah 31. That Sunday night, the preacher and [several of] his people came to see "Nelson's dying sailor," as he was called; and "the ray of hope to his trembling soul and emaciated body was a little increased."

> On Monday evening, many pious men visited the terrified sailor. Their exhortations and explanations of faith made him seek and pray—and he now converted, by divine grace! By this pious minister and his plain, devout members, G. C. S. was so kindly visited until, when partially recovered, he was able to crawl to the chapel. As the report of *Nelson's sailor* had gone through all the streets of Reading, crowds of people came to hear him in the pulpit tell what the Lord had done for his soul.

In Smith's late seventies, when reflecting on his "Reading Sailor Miracle of Grace," he was struck by the likeness to certain details in Acts 9:

> A plain Ananias (called Weller) being directed to visit this dying sailor, it seemed as if the Lord said to him, as he did respecting the chief of sinners, Saul of Tarsus: "Go thy way, for he is a chosen vessel unto me to bear my name before the Gentiles!" Then was Saul certain days with the disciples at Damascus. And so was G. C. Smith with the Christian visitors for some weeks in his sick chamber in Reading, and when recovering, like Saul, preached Christ in the Synagogue.

As for Smith's mother, alone in London and dying of cancer, he could recall how "she frequently said, with crying and tears, that she travailed in birth with my soul more than with all the other five children." She could hardly believe her eyes when she received the good news in writing from Reading, signed, "Your restored and redeemed prodigal." Her first response was to send "a special messenger to Reading, to ascertain the truth of the report. She learned, on his return, that her prayers for twenty-one years were answered, and departed to her Savior in peace." Smith then went to London to bury his mother at Tottenham Court Road Chapel ground, where his father, too, was buried.

However grateful Smith was that his mother lived long enough to hear of his conversion, he knew she had even higher hopes. In 1797, while the *Agamemnon* lay at anchor at Spithead, Smith's mother had come from London to visit her son. He relates:

> Once, she brought with her the Narrative drawn up by the Reverend John Newton of his marvelous escapes and his wonderful conversion to God. This book she affectionately presented to me, with the ardent prayer that I might become, like Newton, a preacher of the gospel to perishing sinners . . . I laughed heartily at the idea of becoming "a methodist parson." I declared that I hoped one day to "bear up" for the port of heaven, yet as to "preaching," it was out of the question. "Anything but that, mother!" She sighed heavily and humbly replied, "There is nothing too hard for the Lord." He who taught her to pray thus, would often answer after a mother's death. "As to the rest of my children," she added, "they are now chiefly settled in the world. Yet from you, my son, I often have hope. You are yet young; your heart is yet tender."

It might not be surprising that Smith's mother, knowing of Newton's history, maintained faith that her son would one day also become a great preacher of the gospel. Both had become steeped in the seamy side of life in a man-of-war after being forcibly pressed into naval service. Both had also, from birth, been the subjects of constant prayer by their mothers. Smith never met Newton personally but he would later frequently quote him and write about him. As for Nancy Smith, though she never lived to see her dream fulfilled, she could nonetheless rejoice that her son had—in Reading, Berkshire—reached his "Damascus."

For more about the linkage between George Charles Smith and John Newton, see this book's Addendum.

CHAPTER 4
NEW SAILING ORDERS
(1803-1809)

After five weeks at Reading, Smith recovered sufficiently from his near fatal illness to make his way back to London during the summer of 1803. Here, the young twenty-one-year-old was able to obtain the same kind of secular employment as before. By autumn, however, he had become "accustomed to engage in prayer meetings and some occasional public speaking in a humble way." Meanwhile, he was on the lookout for more work. Then, "by a most unexpected event," he met a merchant in London who resided near Billingsgate Market. He goes on to relate, "I was then at once engaged for and directed to Bath, to superintend the wine trade of the York House Hotel."

In the promising situation of "cellar superintendent" at this fashionable Bath hotel, Smith continued through the winter. At the same time he was able to "find fellowship" at the Baptist Chapel in nearby Somerset Street. One day, a large prayer meeting was underway. Smith later recalls: "My singular and unexpected engagement at that meeting in the vestry was the means, in the hands of God, of introducing me to an acquaintance with a most respectable deacon and local preacher of that chapel, Opie Smith, Esq., of Westfield House [about a mile from Bath]."

This "other Smith" would come to make a unique impact on the future life of the former Nelson sailor. Opie Smith had already become known as a significant figure in both the brewing industry and the Baptist denomination. When his wife became seriously ill, Opie Smith sold his business in order to focus more fully on furthering the Baptist cause in the southwest of England. As to Somerset Street Chapel, George Charles

Smith recorded that his "constant attendance there at 6 a.m. prayer meetings on Sabbath days, and visits at Westfield Home to breakfast with Opie Smith [would prove to be] of the utmost importance to my soul." Smith goes on:

> In [my own] York Hotel private room, I spent hours in Scripture reading and importunate wrestling prayer, entreating that the Lord would most graciously set before me an "open door" for preaching the gospel to the poor somewhere, and devoting my whole soul and time to seeking for lost sinners, such as I had been, and bringing them to the cross of Christ. This daily ardent prayer for deliverance from the worldly pleasure of a great and celebrated tavern [was] at last answered. The God of all grace led Mr. Opie Smith to "invite my preaching occasionally," when I could obtain liberty [to do so] in some neighbouring village. He provided a horse and went with me. In the early part of 1804, I was afflicted, and for a few days confined to my bed. One morning, Opie Smith visited me—and standing at the foot of my bed, he observed, you must consider, my dear friend, that in the 107th Psalm and the 7th verse, it is written, "He led them forth by the right way." It was a rough way. And so will the Lord lead you, perhaps in a rough way through the wilderness, but in a right way to the Canaan of heaven.

Opie Smith's original concern for the county of Cornwall had been aroused by accounts in a fellow Baptist's missionary periodical, written by Dr. John Rippon. Here, Rippon had described "the destitution in this Druidical county, where idol gods were originally so abundantly worshipped." He arranged with Dr. John Ryland, of the Baptist College in Bristol, to send more Baptist clergy there. In this connection, as George Charles Smith later put it:

> Opie Smith was directed of God, I have no doubt, privately to propose my engaging in the ministry, and going to Bristol Academy as a student of the ministry, or else going under the tuition of some able minister, and a suitable place for preaching. After much serious consideration and prayer, I preferred *private tuition* and active *preaching* anywhere around.

Mr. Opie Smith, soon afterwards, being on a visit to Cornwall and Devon for the establishment of some Christian churches and chapels, stopped at Plymouth Dock [later known as "Devonport"]. Here, he most kindly engaged with the eminent and blessed minister, the Rev. Isaiah Birt, pastor of Morrice Square Chapel, for my tuition, and a chapel at Saltash for my preaching. He most benevolently engaged to send me £20 per annum for my support, until I could obtain a salary somewhere as a settled minister. So I determined, in the autumn of 1804, to resign my responsible station in the York House Hotel, Bath, although I had then a very handsome salary, and a first-rate mode of living.

When I proposed resigning the service under the managers of the hotel concerns, [one of these], Mr. Riley, stormed at me. The winter season, which was the great Bath *harvest*, was now approaching. But I persisted to resign. [In order to obtain] the sanction to enter the ministry from the humble church to which I belonged at Reading, I visited London. Then I traveled to Plymouth Dock, as a preacher with a plain lodging room in Prince's Street, to attend upon Mr. Birt for daily instruction. [I also] proceeded to Saltash [four miles] by boat, on the river Tamar. Or, I walked to the Ferry [where the Albert Bridge was later built], and preached there to the poor on the Lord's day and once a week.

[It was strange] to recollect that I had landed at Plymouth Dock in 1800, from the wreck of a great ship of war, in which I and a crew of nearly five hundred men had almost perished on the French coast. And how I had participated in the sinful pleasures of this great seafaring neighbourhood. And [then] to be astonished at the wonders of divine grace that could save such a sinner as me. And by means of Opie Smith, of Bath, send me as a converted preacher of the gospel to labour in preaching Christ crucified at Saltash, Botus Fleming, Callington, Calstock, and other places [like] Dartmouth and Brixham in South Devon. And [finally], by means of Plymouth Dock, to prepare me for my settlement at Penzance, as pastor of a Christian church.

GEORGE CHARLES SMITH OF PENZANCE

Was George Charles Smith's choice of education for ordained ministry the most advantageous in his particular case? It is difficult to know. There is no question that Smith's six years at sea had already given him an "informal" education that would prove indispensable. More debatable is what academic and social skills Smith may have lost by rejecting the "formal" option he was offered at the Baptist seminary in Bristol. Smith never seems to have doubted his own choice of three years of tutorial theory, supplemented by ministerial practice. He had little patience with any form of higher education that might risk leaving him to the same fate as "dissipated youths at college, training up for the bottomless pit," as he put it.

While maintaining his "daily instruction" with Reverend Birt, Smith was, at the same time, his tutor's "assistant preacher." Both at his primary charge—the Baptist Chapel at Saltash—and at other water-bordered preaching points, which meant mixing with a mostly maritime population. According to Smith, they included "sailors, dockyardmen, fishermen, and watermen," as well as their families. Understandably, they responded positively to the ministry of one who came from a seafaring background, intimately familiar with both their community's privations and exploitations. None knew this advantage better than Opie Smith and Isaiah Birt when the time came for George Charles Smith to take over his own ministry, at England's westernmost port of Penzance.

Over the years, the name "Penzance" would become an inherent part of the life of the one who became known as its "Boatswain Pastor." In public perception, Penzance has long held a reputation for the bizarre combination of pirates and palm trees. The port was, in fact, frequently raided by Barbary pirates right up to the eighteenth century. Since the end of the nineteenth century, this connection has been immortalized by Gilbert and Sullivan's operetta, *The Pirates of Penzance*. As for palm trees, Penzance, with England's mildest, most Mediterranean climate, has always been known for its rich, subtropical vegetation—not least on display in its downtown's Morrab Gardens. Due largely to the city's fame as a popular resort, the population of Penzance almost tripled during the first half of the nineteenth century.

Penzance has, in its very name, also a "religious" association. Made up of "Pen" (Cornish for head or headland) and "Sans" (holy), this "Holy Headland" refers to the ancient chapel site now occupied by Saint Mary's Church on Chapel Street, overlooking the harbor and the grand sweep of Mount's Bay from the west. The alternative meaning of a "Holy Head" has until recently been featured in a portrayal of the severed head of John the Baptist in Penzance's coat of arms. It is still used in the official seal of the town council.

Many local legends maintain that Christ himself visited these parts as a youth, serving on a ship run by his mother Mary's uncle, Joseph of Arimathea. Tradition also holds that his ship may have called at Mount's Bay, where tin—dug from the mines surrounding Penzance—was frequently loaded for the Mediterranean. That possibility has been kept alive to this day in the hymn, so widely known and loved, by William Blake: "And did those feet in ancient times walk upon England's mountains green?"

At the turn of the nineteenth century, there were still signs of robust religious interest in southwestern England, and Penzance was no exception. Seeking to make the most of this, Opie Smith had, in 1802, initiated the first Baptist sanctuary in Penzance. That year—for the sum of £312—he facilitated the purchase of a chapel. This had originally been built in 1788–1789 by the Independents, known from its shape as "The Octagon," and located "near the Morrab Fields, below the North Parade." After serving from 1802 to 1807, the first Baptist preacher there, Reverend Samuel Saunders, a graduate of the Baptists' Bristol Academy, left for a new assignment.

In the spring of 1807, Opie Smith secured an invitation from the Baptist congregation in Penzance to invite his nautical namesake and friend from Plymouth Dock down "on probation for a few weeks." Reverend Isaiah Birt of Morrice Square was happy to cooperate—as he had been by placing his earlier associate Saunders there in 1802. However, no one could have been more satisfied than the Octagon Chapel's own members. They could now record their "gladness for the pleasing and unexpected change" in the pastorless church at the arrival of George Charles Smith.

On May 6, 1807, the congregation sent Smith a letter of call: "When we looked into the villages, we beheld multitudes pressing to hear the word of life drop from your lips. When we look on the church in this place, and behold that which was, a short time since, anarchy and confusion, over the loss of our beloved Brother Saunders, we now see peace and happiness. We therefore hereby give you an invitation to assume the ministerial and pastoral office over us—without a dissenting voice—believing this is the Lord's will."

In his response, Smith underscored his incompetence as "the weakest and unworthiest of our Lord's servants." Yet, he added, "Having sincerely consulted the divine will, I do believe it to be of the Lord. In this opinion, I am greatly strengthened by your worthy patron, Mr. Opie Smith, and my venerable tutor, Rev. Isaiah Birt."

Accordingly, on October 28, 1807, George Charles Smith was ordained and settled as Pastor of the Baptist Octagon Chapel of Penzance. The charge was given to him by his pastoral tutor from Luke 12:43: "It will be good for that servant whom the Master finds so doing when he returns." The congregations at both the day's services were "large and attentive, and several of the ministers and persons present remarked it was 'one of the happiest days they had ever spent.'" For the new and busy Baptist pastor, his prayer was that he might be found incessantly spreading the Lord's kingdom—and "so doing" to his very last day.

Smith's official installation in Penzance did not alter the direction of his ministry. Rather, it helped affirm it. His labors were not limited to his local primary chapel. He continued "preaching to fishermen and sailors all around the coast of Mount's Bay" whenever the occasion offered. According to one report, even before his ordination in 1807, Smith's various congregations could be "numbering often from six hundred to a thousand souls."

By 1809, Smith could claim he had "received grace to minister to both mariners and their dependents during five years, from Torbay to the Land's End, on the South Devon and Cornwall coast." Through the patronage of Opie Smith, this reformed sailor seemed to have obtained the kind of "open door" he had so often implored of his Lord back in Bath. Nonetheless, Smith himself was the first to insist that, in principle, "there was nothing extraordinary in it, as other ministers in coastal districts did the same."

Doubtless, Smith's "natural energies and constitutional activity" did drive him to great lengths. Yet, until 1809, Smith's ministry among seafarers was—like that of his coastal colleagues—really only a part of his "general" ministry. He was, in other words, like Captain John Newton, his mother's model for him, still only a "sailor minister," not yet a "sailors' minister."

Then came a memorable afternoon in early 1809. Seeking to fulfill his ordination charge—to be ever more "so doing"—Smith had been asking his Lord precisely how he could "do more," especially for fellow people of the sea. He has recorded the progress of the conversation that happened while walking down Chapel Street, near Penzance harbor. Suddenly hailed by a couple of sailors, eagerly waving their hats to him while making their way uptown from the quay, he was asked by one of them: "Will you please come on board our vessel, and preach a sermon to us?" "Preach a sermon!" exclaimed Smith in amazement. "How came you to think of asking me?"

Their conversation continued:

> "Why, sir, we belong to the revenue cutter *Dolphin*, and we have been out in such a dreadful gale of wind that every soul expected to perish; our captain is brought on shore very ill, and we thought to have a sermon on board when we came in."
>
> "Where does your vessel lay?"
>
> "In Guavas Lake, sir, here out on the Bay."
>
> "Will your officer allow me to come on board and preach?"
>
> "O yes, sir, he told us to ask."
>
> "Well, this is very singular. I have often wished to preach on board ship, but have never done such a thing. However, if you will bring

your boat on shore for me to-morrow afternoon, I will very gladly
go off with you to preach."

The large revenue cutter *Dolphin* was well known in Cornish waters. She had been kept on the alert constantly in those parts in order to
prevent local smuggling operations—"one of the notorious customs of
Cornwall." On this particular occasion, the *Dolphin* had been at St. Ives
and heard of some desperate smugglers near Basset's Cove who frequented Hell's Bay, as it was called. Here, she barely managed to escape "the
most tremendous hurricane" by casting her guns overboard and hastening
round the Longships Lighthouse off Land's End. Apparently, the crew,
appalled by their narrow escape, had begun to talk of their need for "a
little religion."

A seafarer from the neighboring fishing village of Newlyn—where
Smith had often preached—had then proposed inviting on board "a
preacher at the Octagon Chapel, in Penzance, who had been a sailor."
Still "perfectly astonished" at this initiative, Smith was duly rowed on
board the next day, as agreed. Here, he was received "with great kindness" by the chief officer and led below to where an open space had been
cleared and all hands assembled. Smith had with him a preacher trainee
from Bath, Mr. Shell, whom Opie Smith had sent for tuition at the Penzance Chapel.

As for the worship service itself, Smith could later relate: "My soul
was deeply affected in preaching to these sailors, from Jonah 1:6—'So
the shipmaster came to him and said unto him, What meanest thou,
O sleeper? Arise, call upon thy God! If so be that God will think upon
us, that we perish not.' It was a most affecting time, in remembrance of
storms and tempests at sea, and sins and snares ashore, when I had myself
been a thoughtless sailor in a ship of war." Finally, the service was closed
with prayer by Smith's student assistant.

As they were being rowed back to land, Smith continues, "I said,
'Well, of all the ships I knew or heard of when I was at sea, I never knew
of but one religious sailor in a man-of-war—as we were then without
hope, and without God, in a ship of 500 men, called a Floating Hell,
and no man cared for our souls.'" That "one religious sailor" was Thomas

Doeg, a quartermaster on the *Agamemnon,* who, Smith stated later in his magazine, was one of the influences that eventually brought him to faith.

As the men from the *Dolphin* continued rowing back to land, Smith relates how "the man pulling with the stroke or first oar cried out, in his Cornish dialect, 'Maester, I know one of thy religion in a man-of-war now.' I was so much surprised, that I asked what he meant by 'my religion.' His answer was, 'Why one of your Methodie men.' As this was the general term for a religious person, I entreated him to get me his name, and the ship to which he belonged, and where she was."

The sailor with whom Smith was talking "promised he would when the boat got on shore at the Quay, as he knew a relative of the religious sailor, who was residing in Penzance. He obtained the information I needed, after which I wrote him—begging to know if he was acquainted with any other man who possessed the grace of God." That stroke oar, Hannibal Curnoe, came from the village of Ludgvan, which was near Marazion, between St. Ives and Penzance. Curnoe would soon become a "most zealous" member of Smith's Octagon Chapel. However, his voluntary information about a "Methodie" man on a ship-of-war led to results Curnoe could hardly have imagined. As Smith put it fifty years later: "This commenced the greatest work in all my life, the first Religious Mission among Sailors."

In 1967, Leonard Martin Richards of Madron, Penzance, who was a direct descendent of Hannibal Curnoe, summed up—in an interview with the author—his impression from many years of personal research: "George Charles Smith was a real firebrand man of action, just like an Old Testament prophet!"

CHAPTER 5
CASTING OFF!
(1809–1814)

Delighted at the news Hannibal Curnoe could give him, Smith "determined to prosecute a correspondence with all naval ships where a pious sailor was to be found." He did so with an energy and enthusiasm that had already become his hallmark wherever he went. The first maritime mission task to which Smith now realized he was called would later become known as the "Naval Correspondence Mission." After receiving Curnoe's information, Smith recorded how the dimensions of the challenge began to grow out of control:

> I wrote immediately to [the sailor at] Portsmouth, and received a kind and affectionate answer, begging I would correspond with him. I wrote again to ask if he had any more sailors on board who loved our Lord Jesus Christ. His reply informed me, there was a pious marine on board. I then wrote to the marine, and inquired if he knew of any other religious sailors in the navy. He informed me concerning the *Royal George*, 100 guns. I wrote to this ship, and the sailor [there] corresponded with me, and informed me of the *Royal Oak*, 74. I wrote here also, and heard of the *Zealous*, 74, and the *Elizabeth*, 74.

Smith goes on to recount how sailors on board these ships first told about the *Ganges*, 74. His correspondence with that ship then directed him to the *Tonnant*, of eighty guns, where he received news of not only the *Repulse*, 74, and the *Conqueror*, also 74, but likewise several frigates, sloops-of-war, tenders, and cutters. How was a former man-of-war's man to deal with such a situation as this—suddenly thrust upon him without precedence or the slightest sign of abating?

Smith's immediate involvement was a natural response to his first contact with the Christian cell group movement at sea. As such, it had roots going all the way back to the Early Church. The book of Acts describes how small Christian communities banded together in the face of an overwhelming counterculture. Through these so-called house churches, early converts found both a means of mutual survival and a mission base from which to reach others. During the Napoleonic Wars, a maritime version of this cell group movement had—unknown to Smith—already spontaneously begun in the British wartime navy.

As he recovered from his initial amazement, it became clear to Smith that two considerations would now make some form of "follow-up" work completely vital. The first was pastoral in nature; the second was connected to public relations.

From a pastoral perspective, here was literally a floating flock, "scattered abroad, as sheep without a shepherd." In addition to the dispersion due to sea life itself, there was the religious prejudice often shown by both officers and crew. Smith heard constantly of those who were religiously inclined, where "petty officers were broke, midshipmen disrated, [and] men were selected on the slightest pretence and flogged." In his handwritten responses to these men, Smith reminded them of the importance of the biblical basis for salvation by "free grace alone" and of the necessity for sharing this with their coworkers. In some cases, he even wrote respectfully to an officer on board, requesting freedom of worship for victimized fellow seafarers.

As his correspondence ministry gathered momentum and "hosts of letters" began to arrive, Smith became frustrated. First, there was the sheer workload. In his parsonage, Smith found himself receiving up to fourteen letters a day, a large number at that time. He enlisted "five or six persons to copy and distribute what he wrote." Even more difficult was the financial impact. Expenses for mailing were overwhelming. An early postage debt of £50 drew protests from Smith's young wife.

This developed into a problem that would plague him throughout his long career—expenses way ahead of any hopes of income.

At the same time, Smith soon realized that this Naval Correspondence Mission also needed to serve a second purpose—public relations. How could the church serve seafarers without developing an adequate base, both for prayer support and funding? In that sense, Smith began to glimpse a greater role for the Christian church at sea than merely to provide pastoral follow-up ministry.

This publicity challenge seemed at first overwhelming. As Smith himself expressed it, "I was indeed like the woman of Samaria—I could not contain this good news, but ran around with those letters, reading them for weeks to all descriptions of persons, and expressing my amazement that God should begin such a work as this in the navy. I found many ministers and persons [responding] very calmly, 'Ah, it is all very well if they last.' Others actually declared, 'It's all empty profession, we don't believe there can be any religion in a man-of-war.' Some even laughed at me."

In Smith's own congregation in Penzance, too, there were members who began to complain, saying, "We can hear nothing now at that chapel but about sailors." In some quarters, there were even insinuations about subversion by "sectarians." However, for Smith there was never a question of giving up. He forged ahead while at the same time enlisting an impressive series of sponsors. Among these was Lady Mary Grey, the spouse of Captain Sir George Grey, commissioner of the Naval Dockyard at Portsmouth. There was also William Henry Hoare, the well-known Fleet Street banker. Like several others of Smith's initial supporters, both became early advocates for the distribution of Scripture among naval personnel.

It was not long before Smith discovered he was not alone in promoting the spiritual welfare of seafarers. Besides the concern of a growing number of fellow ministers of different denominations, Smith became aware of the naval work of preexisting national agencies like the Naval and Military Bible Society (NMBS), the British and Foreign Bible Society (BFBS), and the Religious Tract Society (RTS). Besides cooperating with these, Smith began sending a selection of his sailors' letters to the religious press for publication, as well as to individual ministers for use as sermon illustrations.

Among the earlier letters Smith published was one forwarded to him by a clergyman at Plymouth Dock. It was written by "a common seaman" signing himself "J. C.," and addressed to John Hubback, a Methodist "master's mate" on HMS *Elizabeth* (then off Lisbon). "The date is observable," Smith points out, "because the letter is dated HMS *Ganges,* 7 April 1809, showing how Bible study cell groups were already well under way at the time of the *Dolphin* incident that year." Here, J. C. thanks the Lord Jesus Christ for his great mercy toward both himself and Hubback as a fellow believer. He goes on to remind about the Lord's prediction of persecution for all who follow him. At the same time, he sees good reason for "in nothing being terrified, knowing that all power in heaven and earth is given to our Lord and Master."

Smith underscores how J. C. was "blessed to the conversion of several of the crew, forming a large society, which has since been drafted into several ships where the Gospel was previously unknown." Such movement was, in part, due to "the folly of anti-Christian officers." As in the early church, those who persecuted lost out to "the wisdom of God." As new believers increased on new ships, fresh crews were "brought to a knowledge of the truth, and the officers heard, to their utter astonishment, that their ship [too] was tainted with Methodism. The more noise they made, the more religion flourished."

Before long, the open manner and "almost apostolic vein" of these letters were producing "the most wonderful effects," particularly in London and Edinburgh. The British sailor was, after all, highly redeemable! This encouraged Smith to start on a second major mission endeavor in 1811—compiling a so-called nautical dialogue. Its purpose would be to combine Smith's own sea experience with this emerging form of naval correspondence.

This particular type of literature had already been introduced by Dr. Robert Hawker, the vicar of Charles in Plymouth. With his ties to the navy, Hawker had been deputy chaplain of the Plymouth garrison since

1797. By then he had a reputation as "one of the most popular preachers in the kingdom," with devotional literature for the poor as a priority. In 1806 and 1810 he produced a two-part autobiography entitled *The Sailor Pilgrim*. Although generally well received, both his style and content seemed unduly complicated—in contrast to Smith's spicy dialogue with its aroma of tar and salt water.

The project Smith now developed was entitled, "The Boatswain's Mate: A Dialogue between Two British Seamen." It was made up of several parts. The first two were written "in a small room at Chapel Street, Penzance," and the first of these was published in 1811–1812 in the religious newspaper, *The Instructor*. The November 1817 edition of *The Evangelical Magazine* hailed their publication in book form that year as a highly promising event. It expressed hope that the "very free use of the dialect peculiar to British seamen" would continue to attract land folk no less than seafaring folk.

During the next couple of years, five additional parts were published, making up a seven-part book that would ultimately go through repeated reprints both in Britain and America. As late as in 1886, Captain R. W. Wilson, who in younger years had been "personally acquainted" with George Charles Smith, provided the preface of yet another edition of *The Boatswain's Mate*—then in a slightly abridged form, on behalf of what was at that time the Mission to Deep Sea Fishermen.

The general theme of the series is the faith journey of two tars in Britain's Napoleonic War navy. Meeting in the street at Plymouth Dock, Bob, the Boatswain's Mate on HMS *Dreadnought*, opens the book by hailing a fellow sailor, James, Quarter Master on HMS *Royal George*, with the words: "Yoho, shipmate, what ship? From whence came you?" The jovial Bob's drinking and revelry are put on hold as he agrees to continue his conversation with the believer James in nearby Stoke Fields. After a series of blasphemous protests, Bob finds himself strongly influenced by the dramatic details of James' life and subsequent conversion.

With that introduction, Smith goes on to convey the most important events and conversations from his own career in the wartime navy. These include his drunken brawl in the theatre in London, narrow escapes at sea, the Battle of Copenhagen, and his illness at Yarmouth. Finally, he recounts his dramatic conversion experience in Reading—in answer to his frail mother's prayers. The whole narrative is full of fascinating facts from the spiritual awakening that swept through all ranks in the early nineteenth century British Navy. The text also integrates much of Smith's naval correspondence experiences, including the hostile reactions to Bible study meetings on shipboard.

With *The Boatswain's Mate* continuing to be so popular both on ship and shore, the book served a dual evangelistic purpose: people at sea started to realize that they, too, could be spiritually transformed and people ashore began believing that missionary outreach could actually promote that kind of change—while some even came to see their own need for conversion.

In 1812, Smith found he had to go to London on a preaching trip. As he explained, his immediate purpose was "to obtain assistance to discharge a debt upon the Octagon Chapel in Penzance." To that end, he had been directed to call on Alderman John Wilson in the latter's counting house in Cheapside. At first, Smith was somewhat offended by the Alderman's brusque manner, and asked for the return of his book of commitments. "I did not come here to insult or to be insulted," he said. Suddenly, Wilson realized who Smith was. "Did you not write the dialogue about Bob and James in the *Instructor* newspaper?" That did it. He asked Smith to preach the following week at the two renowned chapels that were currently under Wilson's management.

In this way, a delighted Smith was given the opportunity to preach from the former pulpits of George Whitefield—in not only the Tabernacle, but also the Tottenham Court Road chapel. As other London chapels now also opened their pulpits, he would later look back to the summer of 1812 as the year of his "entry on the London scene." Somewhat ruefully, he would compare this with his failed attempt to enter that scene quite literally—at the Surrey Theater one decade earlier.

CHAPTER 6
CONTINENTAL CROSSWINDS
(1814-1816)

After Smith cast off in answer to the Lord's call in 1809, he came to see himself sailing into sea-related work that God had already prepared for him "in advance"—in accordance with Ephesians 2:10. Naturally, he had no idea where this might lead to. He first found himself navigating new waters with his Naval Correspondence Mission and his book, *The Boatswain's Mate*. After that, he ran into "crosswinds." As it proved, these would draw him for a while elsewhere—first over to the continental mainland of Western Europe, then out to a group of islands in the English Channel.

During the fall of 1813, a violent storm forced a British transport vessel to take refuge in the port of Penzance. The ship was involved in repatriating French military prisoners of war from San Sebastian to Brest. These former enemies turned out to be eager for the French tracts and Scriptures that Smith was able to offer.

Smith saw this event as a dual call to action. First, he launched a literature mission to Spain and especially France—ravaged by war and contaminated with the "infidel" writings of Voltaire and Rousseau. By so doing, he sought to help "convert the energies of their ardent minds from the wild project of subjugating Europe, to the noble and sublime scheme of aiding Britain in . . . subduing the world beneath the feet of the 'Prince of Peace.'" Secondly, Smith saw this as an opportunity to minister to British soldiers in the field as well as British sailors in foreign ports.

In early March 1814, armed with a large stock of Bibles, Testaments, and tracts, Smith embarked for Pasajes in Spain, close to the Franco-

Spanish border. Then—from the Pyrenees to Paris—he continued for nearly five months with voluntary chaplaincy in the wake of Wellington's Peninsular Army. He even received praise from the general himself for his ministry among wounded British soldiers. He also managed to reach out to British sailors in the ports of Pasajes, Bordeaux, Calais, and Marseilles. In this way, Smith's activity became a prelude to his subsequent involvement in international seafarers' mission.

On the wider scene, the roving pastor from Penzance also promoted the post-war French Methodist Mission. In conjunction with the British and Foreign School Society, he was even able to help introduce the new "Lancasterian School System" into France. Named after the English Quaker, Joseph Lancaster, this educational system became popular in the early nineteenth century as a cheap means of multiplying early education by making abler pupils monitors or helpers among their fellow students.

By the time Smith returned to England in July 1814, Bonaparte had been banished to Elba and it seemed the war was over. However, new needs immediately appeared on Smith's horizon. Penzance is known as "The Gateway to the Scilly Isles," a group of islands in the English Channel, some twenty-six miles due west of Land's End. Smith now found himself responding to the rampant poverty that had recently been escalating in this isolated area.

The Scilly Isles have a history going back as far as to biblical times. Historians believe that Phoenician traders used Scilly as a port of call on their voyages to Cornwall to load tin. Shortly before the year 1000, King Olaf Tryggvasson of Norway is recorded to have visited Scilly and was, according to tradition, converted to Christianity by the help of a hermit living there. The king then left to campaign for his newfound faith in his Scandinavian homelands, offering the dire alternatives of being baptized or slaughtered!

Over the years, island inhabitants came to depend more and more on occupations such as fishing, kelp gathering, and—especially on the "off-islands" beyond the "parent" island, St. Mary's—wrecking, and smuggling. A reported local addition to the church litany read: "We pray thee, O Lord, not that wrecks should happen, but that if any wrecks do happen, Thou wilt guide them into the Scilly Isles for the benefit of the poor inhabitants."

The Scillies were notorious for the deadly rocks and unpredictable currents that surrounded them. These "Isles of the Blest," as the Celts called them, provided many shipwrecks, often characterized as "God's blessings." As to smuggling, with such a high level of British duty on French imports, the practice grew into a major local industry, one which even clergy were known to condone.

Toward the close of the Napoleonic War, the Scilly Islands met with escalating troubles. Smuggling virtually came to an end, with the introduction of fast coastguard cutters and a general renewal of the "Preventive Service" around the Scillies. In addition, successive crop failures resulted in widespread famine. Conditions were further aggravated by constant neglect and poor administration by local authorities.

"Being the resident minister of Penzance, Cornwall," Smith wrote later, "I was within thirty leagues of the islands, to which a packet regularly sailed every week. I had often been requested to establish preaching on those islands. Previous to 1814, the Reverend J. T. Jeffrey, who was one of my assistant preachers to the villages, went over to Scilly, and returned with such accounts, that I was determined to establish a mission there." Jeffrey would continue serving the Scilly Islands for more than seven years. To secure a source of support, Smith cofounded the Baptist Home Missionary Society, which eventually became a pioneer among home mission societies everywhere.

In 1815, Smith sailed off to investigate the situation together with "a respectable Quaker of Penzance," two leading local Methodists, and Reverend Jeffrey. "We went from home to home," he wrote. "The scenes were most harrowing and dreadful—the people were actually dying from want of food. We were occupied nearly a week; and returning to St. Mary's, I preached to an immense congregation in the street, by appointment, when I described what we had seen and heard in the off-islands. . . . On our return to Penzance, I sent the account to our two Cornish newspapers, and the publication of them excited general alarm and enquiry."

Meanwhile, the local Anglican pastor in Scilly saw this as an affront. He published an indignant denial, saying he had seen "no distress in the islands." His allegation was confirmed by the lieutenant governor, and these two managed to win over the local county magistrates on the mainland. As a result, Smith found himself "now seriously dragged into a public warfare with the magistrates and all their adherents, while letters were continually coming from Scilly that the people were perishing."

Shortly afterwards, however, published reports of the lieutenant governor's abuse of "a poor girl he had seduced at Scilly," coupled with his chronic misuse of alcohol, silenced him. Moreover, the magistrates visited the Scillies themselves and could soon corroborate all of Smith's statements. After returning to Penzance, they sent a unanimous vote of thanks to Smith for his perseverance. In London, Smith reprinted his reports in book form, while also promoting a national society for providing aid to the population of Scilly. During his fundraising campaign in the capital, Smith succeeded in enlisting not only the support of several naval officers, but also the help of the slave trade abolitionist, William Wilberforce, and even the patronage of the Prince Regent.

In the course of three years of "labours for the Scilly Islands," Smith sailed there several times. First, he arranged to bring to the islands several casks of barley, oatmeal, pork, and beef, as well as loads of clothing, blankets, and basic medicine. This was crucial for the many hurting inhabitants, especially in the off-islands. Smith's efforts to provide preaching, Scripture distribution, and new sabbath and weekday schools also made a significant difference. As a token of their gratitude, the citizenry of Hugh Town, St. Mary's, crowded at the end of the pier on one occasion and lit up a tar barrel, so their benefactor could see a huge flag as he sailed away. On it they had inscribed the words "SMITH FOR EVER!"

A major step toward more long-term relief was when Smith helped start a local microenterprise—a project that enabled the women of Scilly to generate their own income. It began with a "respectable committee of tradesmen and genteel females," meeting at an inn in Hugh Town. There, they established an "Industrious Society," the main object of which was to produce lambs' wool stockings. The prince regent agreed to become the Society's Royal Patron. He was, according to Smith, "much pleased" with their gift of "two handsome pairs" of hose, ordering them "into the care of the keeper of his wardrobe." Eventually, other women were engaged in preparing twine and nets, to help toward the recovery of the traditional Scillonian fishing industry.

In a work published in 1828 on *The Scilly Islands and the Famine,* Smith gives a graphic account of how, despite accusations to the contrary, he received "not one farthing" for his personal expenses and labors during that terrible time. He wrote in that connection, "This business of Scilly taught me such a lesson concerning the importance of perseverance and public opinion, as I shall never forget." Unfortunately, Smith never learned the additional lesson of keeping accurate accounts during his Scilly Islands Mission. Though there was never the slightest evidence of any personal dishonesty, this failing would be repeated in other contexts in years to come, thus causing endless embarrassment in both the public and private arena.

CHAPTER 7
"AQUATIC PREACHING"
(1817)

Before focusing on his continental and Scilly Island missions, "George Charles Smith" had already become a catchword in the city of London for intentional mission outreach to the maritime world. In 1812, as the author of *The Boatswain's Mate*, he had found himself preaching both in Whitefield's chapels and elsewhere in the capital. That year, he was also invited to preach "by general public advertisement" at what became his first major sermon delivered specifically to seafarers.

The event was arranged by Dr. John Rippon, a Baptist leader famous for his widely used hymnal. His church, Carter Lane Baptist Chapel, was located in a notorious sector of London's "Sailortown"—Tooley Street in Rotherhithe. Rippon knew about the kind of temptations seafarers came up against ashore. He also knew his fellow Baptist Smith's skills and special concerns. He decided to send out posters and fliers to the ships along both banks of the Thames, announcing that the Reverend G. C. Smith from Penzance would be preaching to sailors at the Carter Lane Chapel in the evening of the following "Lord's-day."

That autumn evening in 1812, Rippon also sent torchbearers to help direct all who responded. As a result, the spacious galley that had been reserved for sailors was "completely wedged up." Smith was overwhelmed by the scene. In a stirring sermon, he held forth from Scripture, quoted from sailors' letters, and shared from experiences during his own six years at sea.

The captain of the Tower Hill press gang, sitting in front in full uniform, had told his men that "on such an important religious occasion" no mariner must be molested. After the service, while "hundreds of sailors were in tears," the press captain himself called on Smith in the vestry and said: "I am in an awkward berth for religion, but I am ordered to this post. Thank God," he went on, "that you are a press-master for Jesus Christ. Good night! Take all hands to heaven, if possible!"

The Carter Lane Chapel service led to no immediate organizational result. Nevertheless, the worship service showed what possibilities there were for a preaching ministry among seafarers, not least in a merchant navy capacity. As such, the Carter Lane Chapel event of 1812, although in itself a Baptist initiative, was invaluable as a prelude to the Methodist-linked beginnings of organized maritime mission.

Meanwhile, Smith was still primarily pastor of an expanding but debt-ridden church in Penzance. From here, he continued to combine his pastorate with a fast-growing program of "Home Mission." First, he sponsored several new chapels in villages surrounding Penzance, employing a succession of student preachers. He then developed a "North Devon Sea Coast Mission." Backed by faithful friends, Smith would wend his way with a horse and cart loaded with tracts and Scriptures, through "the darkest villages and sea-ports" all along the coast of Devonshire.

To reach inhabitants who had no church connection, Smith would rely on open-air preaching. Here he experienced a level of persecution very similar to that of Wesley and Whitefield. However, he also met with sufficient encouragement to become a passionate promoter of open-air preaching to the end of his days. With his "stentorian voice" and forceful rhetoric, he was soon being hailed by *The Times* of London as "the prince of field preachers." Smith's activities were eventually recognized as a leading factor in the founding of the "Home Missionary Society" in 1819.

Smith's preoccupation with home mission did not mean he had forgotten sailors. He continued to facilitate Scripture and tract distribution among both British and foreign seafarers. He also carried on itinerant preaching in coastal villages. Through the latter, he showed keen awareness of the long-term sociological impact of such communities. As a result of spiritual neglect, coastal societies might well become "nurseries of godlessness" for people of the sea. Nevertheless, despite his sense of the relevance of "sailors and villages," Smith had, by 1817, still not arrived at any ongoing plan for mission among seafarers as such.

It was not until his arrival in London, during the summer of 1817, that he discovered to his amazement how seafarers themselves—without the aid of any ordained minister—had already improvised a plan for their own spiritual nurture and growth. While preaching at the Carter Lane Baptist Church that summer, Smith had been the guest of one of its leading members, Thomas Phillips—a lighter company owner based at London Bridge. Phillips had by then become a voluntary distributor of religious literature on behalf of the Religious Tract Society. He had a ready field of activity among the many sailors and river men he mingled with as a master lighter man.

In May 1817, a customs friend took Phillips to what he called a "Floating Home of Prayer" in the Lower Pool of the Thames. Here, he discovered scores of officers and men from various colliers meeting on one of them. A blue flag inscribed "Bethel" had flown from the masthead since noon that day. After taking part in prayers and hymn singing, Phillips found that many wanted his tracts. Shortly afterwards, he saw the sheer delight of his houseguest, G. C. Smith, when he invited him to join him and experience the scene for the first time.

Smith's first such "Bethel Meeting" in the summer of 1817 had a prehistory of its own already going back three years. For Smith himself, it was especially meaningful that this particular meeting happened off Rotherhithe on the south bank of the River Thames. For a long time, Rotherhithe had had strong maritime ties, with a name believed to derive from the Saxon word for "Sailors' Haven." Smith could never forget that it was from Rotherhithe, at the Cherry Garden Stairs, that he had shipped out as a 14-year-old cabin boy in the spring of 1796.

In future years, no one was more insistent than this Baptist pastor that the meetings under the Bethel Flag—and indeed the whole Seafarers' Mission Movement—"began, as most good things that require active zeal do, among the *Wesleyan Methodists*; and that *three years* before any member of [any other] denomination had been permitted to put his hand to the work, it was zealously and nobly promoted and advanced by the Wesleyan Methodists at Rotherhithe."

Just as it was the shoemaker William Carey who launched the world mission movement in 1792, so it was a shoemaker called Zebedee Rogers who would come to play a similar role in the seafaring world. In the early summer of 1814, Rogers, who was a member of the Silver Street Wesleyan Methodist Chapel in Rotherhithe, had befriended an unhappy looking seafarer after a service there. He turned out to be David Simpson of North Shields, captain of the collier brig *Friendship*. Rogers invited him to a "class meeting" at his church and writes in an 1827 memoir:

> He [Captain Simpson] invited me on board on his vessel's next voyage. I asked him if he thought his people would come into the cabin and let me pray with them. The captain said, "Go and ask them." I went to the half-deck, and told them they were all wanted in the cabin. "Cabin, sir!" they said with surprise. "Yes, all of you." They all came. I read and prayed with them, and got the captain to pray also. We had one more prayer-meeting that voyage. The next voyage . . . [another] brig laid at the *Friendship's* quarter, and her captain invited me to board her and hold a meeting. From that time I went on until now.

During the months ahead, lay-led prayer meetings increased among the many two-masted brigs carrying coal from North England to the Pool of London's Thames River. Meanwhile, shoemaker Rogers was relieved to be able to transfer follow-up responsibility to his colleague, Samuel Jennings, at the Rotherhithe Chapel. Jennings, a successful local timber merchant, had transformed his stable into an auxiliary meeting place that was often misspelled "the Tempel." Here he addressed the crowds of sailors coming from the coal brigs, eventually earning the Methodist title of a "Local Preacher."

It had by now become clear that a spiritual awakening had begun among merchant seafarers on the river waters of the Metropolis. As such, it followed the Naval Awakening among naval seafarers during the Napoleonic War period. In this sense, the "Thames Revival," led by the coordinated ministries of Rogers and Jennings, represents a new era of maritime mission history. Their joint efforts, from 1814 on, became the first organized and ongoing program of preaching known to have been established anywhere for the special benefit of seafarers.

After a couple of years, it was decided to select a convenient vessel to serve as "host" ship for all interested crews in the vicinity. In order to identify such a ship during the darker days of winter, a lantern would be hoisted at the main masthead. However, as the days of spring lengthened, this "winter signal" was of no use. Instead, the seafarers discussed an alternative in the shape of a flag. The important question was, what *kind* of flag should this be?

George Charles Smith has recorded how Zebedee Rogers was personally involved with the answer to this question. Rogers stated that:

> After much prayer, the word "BETHEL" was deeply impressed upon his soul. He thought this would be a very pretty *bible-word*, but could not imagine what could be the meaning. . . . His sister, to his great surprise had heard a preacher declare that this word in the Old Testament signified the *House of God*. Zebedee Rogers was so delighted that he went to work as soon as possible to collect a few shillings to buy blue and white bunting, and have a flag made with the word "BETHEL" and to have it hoisted as soon as possible at the masthead of a ship in the Lower Pool… [to] signify that a prayer meeting in the evening would be held on that ship.

The early Bethel flag, discovered and promoted by Smith from 1817.
(Chart and Compass, 1914, p. 55)

With the help of seafarers, Rogers' sister was able to obtain the necessary materials and sewed the first "Bethel Flag." The emblem was first hoisted by Captain T. Hindhulph of South Shields on the collier brig *Zephyr*, Sunday afternoon, March 23, 1817. A second Bethel Flag was soon needed, in order to cope with the growing demand.

The word "Bethel" would always remain the distinctive feature of the flag. However, some seafarers decided to add two further symbols— Noah's dove, carrying the olive leaf of peace and the five-pointed star of Bethlehem. In this way, the flag came to symbolize all three major festivals of the Christian year: The star, for the birth of Christ at Christmas, the dove of peace, for the outcome of Calvary at Easter, and the word "Bethel," for the founding of the Christian church at Pentecost.

The hoisting of this banner on those Thames collier brigs opened up horizons no one could have imagined. For decades to come, the Bethel Flag would circle the globe and become not only the symbol, but even the actual means of mission outreach in the seafaring world. No one was destined to play a more important role in facilitating that expansion than George Charles Smith.

The *Zephyr* was the first ship on which the flag had been unfurled earlier that spring. It was also the ship where Smith experienced his first Bethel Meeting. Captain Hindulph was still there to welcome Smith and his hosts, Thomas Phillips and family, on board. Smith recalled the event in the following way:

> The cabin became soon filled with captains and seamen. Some bits of wood were laid across different chests to serve as seats. I stood behind, up in a corner; and while unobserved, I noticed attentively their method of proceeding; the person who had come off from the shore, gave out three verses of a hymn and then prayed. Several captains and seamen successively followed with a short hymn, or prayer . . . I was much impressed with the following: "O thou, that didst call the seamen of Galilee, make bare thine arm and pour down thy blessings on all the captains and mates, seamen and cabin boys, now lying in the river!"

At that, Smith could no longer resist the urge to address them. At first, words failed him from sheer emotion. Finally, he managed to tell how he had once "sailed out of the river as a cabin boy and was now—

through divine grace—a minister of the Lord Jesus Christ." He confessed his astonishment at what he saw God had done—despite "all the temptations abounding on either shore." And he counted it "an honour to stand among them and mingle his prayers and praises with theirs."

The following week, Smith was welcomed back to the *Zephyr* to a far greater gathering, this time to preach on the quarterdeck. He concluded his sermon with a challenge—to be no more ashamed to serve Christ on the river than others were to serve sin at Wapping or Rotherhithe. "You have," he underscored, "for the first time in the history of our country, raised a standard for Christ on the river Thames. May that flag never be struck to any of the enemies of the cross!"

The many that followed up with prayers for the preacher showed that this brother sailor had won the hearts of these Bethel pioneers. That they had won his, too, became increasingly clear in the weeks that followed. Smith's call from the crew of the coast cutter *Dolphin* in 1809 had now been renewed—this time for life. For the rest of Smith's three-month stay in Philips' home in Rotherhithe, there is no record of how far he managed to collect funds for his chapel back in Penzance. But many continued to be stirred by his sermons "on crowded decks" under the Bethel Flag.

Finally, conscious as ever of public relations, Smith decided to offer "the first publicly advertised service on shipboard." This would be a floating counterpart to the seafarers' worship service he had held on shore at Carter Lane Chapel in 1812. Since Bethel Meetings had been centered mainly around Rotherhithe on the south side of the river, Smith wanted to focus on the north side this time, near the Sailortown district of Wapping. When a "chapel-going" ship owner there, Captain Hill, offered the use of his ship, the *Agenoria,* for the event, Smith saw this as providential.

A publicity campaign was launched, with the *Agenoria* ideally moored just off the Wapping shore, close to London Bridge. Leaflets and placards were distributed along both banks of the river, as well as among the tiers of ships at anchor. On the day itself, the response was even more overwhelming than at Carter Lane five years earlier. Philips loaned a large lighter, made fast alongside the ship, so as to help hundreds more stand within earshot. People filled the windows of houses on shore. Many had climbed the rigging of ships nearby. And, as the tide ebbed, crowds swarmed across the beaches.

With the Bethel Flag flying aloft, and "some thousands of hearers," George Charles Smith ascended the three casks placed on the hatchway as a pulpit. His sermon, based on Acts 27:27–29, described sinners suddenly awakened to imminent danger. The vast audience seemed transfixed. As for the metropolitan press, the event was portrayed as a religious sensation. Characterized in the headlines as "Aquatic Preaching," the feasibility of proclaiming the gospel to seafarers on their own element had now been publicly and convincingly demonstrated.

The topic of "religious improvement of seamen" was shortly afterwards reinforced by a second sermon, this time to a crowd of seafarers and landsfolk on the sailing ship *John*. With the autumn evenings now becoming darker, a great awning had been stretched over the deck, with lanterns hung out on the companionway and the capstan. The text was from Matthew 14:30–31. The combined effect of Smith's sermon and the prayers of seafarers present were such that "some infidel young men" who had originally come to jeer decided to "leave the scene in shame."

The result of Smith's summer stay in London was twofold. First of all, he became indisputably "The Sailors' Preacher" of his age. Eventually acclaimed as "the most popular preacher in the kingdom," his status among seafarers remained unique. Although he had never actually sailed as a boatswain, he was by now universally known as "Boatswain Smith," a title he accepted as one of jovial yet genuine affection from his fellow seafarers. Secondly, Smith established "ministerial preaching," not only "lay-led prayer gatherings," as an additional feature of future Bethel Meetings.

CHAPTER 8
LAUNCHING THE LONDON "ARK"
(1818)

"What an excellent plan it would be to have a ship converted into a chapel afloat, and moored in the Thames for constant preaching to sailors!" Smith would later recall that the first time this thought occurred to him was while watching the boatloads of sailors converging on the *Agenoria*. He goes on to assert that from that time the thought never left him.

It is, of course, possible that the idea of a floating chapel may have occurred to others. However, Smith was certainly the first who went to work on it. He was convinced that "this was from God." And for the rest of his stay in London in late 1817, he made sure that the subject of a "permanent pulpit" in the river was "continually brought forth," whether in the pulpit, the vestry, or the parlor. The immediate response was encouraging. Many remarked how seafarers now "leapt with alacrity and delight" alongside ships where a sermon was to be preached. Here they would take their places "on the rigging or gangways, where they felt more at home than they could be in the most elegantly cushioned pews on shore."

Smith observed that many more would have found their way to churches and chapels on land if they had not been deterred by "pewing restrictions," or by those who took offense at the sailor's proverbial "smell of tar." So much greater was the likelihood that sailors would readily fill a sanctuary they could call their own. As the time approached for his return to Penzance, Smith became increasingly impatient. "All approved but no one came forward" to follow up on such a plan, now that Smith himself would soon be so far removed.

It was Smith's friend, Thomas Phillips, who suggested visiting the counting house of Robert Humphrey Marten, a shipbroker and Congregationalist. Phillips hoped that Marten might help contribute to Smith's still needy "chapel case" in Penzance. As they looked at all the posters along the office walls advertising ships for sale, a new thought dawned on Smith's companion: "Here is your man for a floating chapel!"

Smith jumped at Phillips' proposal. As for Marten, a man known for his wisdom and sincerity, he saw at once the sense in such a suggestion, and proposed that someone should draw up a prospectus. Smith immediately countered that Marten himself must be the man. The outcome was that the December 1817 issue of *The Evangelical Magazine* carried, under Marten's name, "Suggestions for the More Effectual Religious Instruction of British Seamen while in Harbour."

A relieved Smith returned to Penzance and immediately went to work on a tract supporting the project. Called *The British Ark*, it carried the following subtitle: *A Brief Narrative of Facts, Leading, by Divine Providence, to an Attempt to Obtain a Floating Place of Worship.* In it, Smith referred to himself as "A Minister of the Everlasting Gospel; once in the Humble Station of a Cabin Boy." Marten, making the most of his city contacts, distributed the tract far and wide. Covering the sequence of events from Smith's first visit on the *Zephyr* to his interview with Marten, the tract became so popular that it was reprinted in several editions.

On January 5, 1818, a group of churchmen and dissenters, led by Lieutenant James E. Gordon RN and supported by William Wilberforce and R. H. Marten, founded the "Committee for the Relief of Distressed Seamen." In the wake of the Napoleonic War, thousands of unemployed seafarers had been roaming the streets of midwinter London, hungry and homeless. As the result of a successful subscription, seven "Receiving Ships" could be rapidly opened along the river, so as to provide needy seafarers with shelter, clothes, food, and rudimentary medical treatment. Smith and Marten decided to combine popular support for this example of maritime social concern with a complementary concern for seafarers' spiritual welfare.

From Penzance, Smith arranged for a "sailor draftsman" to sketch a ship's interior, fitted up as a floating chapel. He sent this, together with other items, to Marten who coordinated a preliminary meeting on February 5, 1818, in order to elect a committee and implement plans for a suitable vessel. Within a month, the *Speedy*, a 379-ton, three-decked sloop of war and veteran of the Napoleonic War Navy, was secured for £700. Smith had already obtained £100. Most of the remainder was provided as an unsolicited loan by George Green, a well-known shipbuilder and ship owner in Blackwall.

Finally, in March of the same year, a public meeting of the Port was held at the City of London Tavern, for the formal founding of The Port of London Society for Promoting Religion among Merchant Seamen (PLS). Although this Society (PLS) was formed primarily for preaching the gospel on board a floating chapel, it was stated that "other plans" were also being considered.

In order to "enliven the meeting and promote the subscription," Smith was invited to introduce a resolution in which the Society disclaimed "all inclination to promote Sectarian Views," and would rather seek "an extended Union of all denominations of Christians." In theory, this opened the way for support by outreach-oriented members of the established Church of England. But in practice, Anglican bishops balked at the notion of their clergy entering into public cooperation with other denominations. It was essentially Congregational and Baptist Dissenters, together with occasional Methodists, who actually took responsibility for the Society.

The Port of London Society of 1818 thereby became the first organization in history devoted to a comprehensive ministry among merchant seafarers—including preaching in a dedicated sanctuary. Prior to this, the only form of organization for the spiritual welfare of seafarers had been by Scripture distribution—not yet by orally proclaiming the gospel to them, as prescribed in Romans 10:14–15.

The task was now to make the recently acquired warship ready for her role as a floating sanctuary. Smith's friend, Benjamin Tanner, a master shipwright from Wapping, was of great help. A former cabin boy himself, he "would not take a farthing" for supervising the refitting. He did so in such a way that visiting sailors felt proud of their new chapel—and above all, at home in it.

While the future *Ark*—as she came to be called—was "fitting out" in Limehouse Dock, Smith made use of his stay in London to gather the shipwrights and workers for the floating chapel's first public prayer service. It concluded with all hands singing the "Doxology." Soon afterwards, she was ready to be towed upriver to her new moorings off Wapping New Stairs. Under way she was accompanied by the cheers of crews on the ships she passed and the crowds of landlubbers who watched along both banks of the river. Finally, on May 14, 1818, she was dedicated at a memorable service—with Smith's childhood pastor, the Reverend Roland Hill, preaching from Genesis 8 about the dove that found no rest elsewhere and therefore returned to the ark.

Interior of the world's first seafarers' church, the former warship Speedy,
rebuilt with the help of Smith in 1818 and known as the Ark.
(Courtesy of The Sailors' Society)

The launching of the *Ark* marked an epoch-making historic event—the opening of "the first seafarers' church in the world." As such, the Port of London Society's floating chapel was the result of the Thames Revival and the birth of the Bethel Movement. To quote a leading personality in late nineteenth century seafarers' mission, "The Thames from the first day it began to flow, never witnessed a greater day in its history than this." Reverend Edward W. Matthews was at that time general secretary of a mission that had grown out of the ministry of the London *Ark*—the British and Foreign Sailors' Society, known today as the Sailors' Society. His familiar big beard eventually earned him the nickname "Father Neptune."

In the beginning, worship attendance on the *Ark* was far from impressive, with less than 200 finding their way to a sanctuary capable of holding close to 800. By August, however, as soon as Smith had arrived from Penzance, momentum began to build. From then on, thirty to forty ships would make fast, and crew members would fill the center and upper deck of the ship, while masters, merchants, and families from shore crowded into the side seats and galleries. After Smith returned to his pastoral duties in Penzance in November, the committee could report that worship attendance had increased by no less than five times.

Smith also continued preaching and counseling at the more informal Bethel Meetings on the colliers in the Lower Pool. With the cooperation of Thomas Phillips, Smith was able to expand those meetings to the Upper Pool. However, this idyllic situation—with Bethel Meetings stimulating and supplementing activities on the Floating Chapel—was not to last. By August of the next year, when Smith returned to Thomas Phillips' home in Horsleydown for a fresh round of preaching engagements, he discovered that "a kind of religious war" had developed on the river.

The main bone of contention was that lay managers of the Port Society's Floating Chapel were demanding that captains of vessels throughout the Pool area of the Thames should renounce their Thursday evening Bethel services. Their aim was to promote attendance on the *Ark*. Collier captains demurred, however, since they had already given up Wednesday nights in favor of Mr. Jennings' mid-week Rotherhithe meetings. Meanwhile, their other weeknight meetings had been flourishing—with up to nine simultaneous meetings of well over one hundred on each ship.

One might, of course, have called this a "good problem." However, the majority of independent-minded seafarers reacted instinctively against what they saw as a clear infringement of their freedom of assembly. Moreover, many simply preferred their freer meeting style to the more formal worship practice of services on the *Ark*.

Smith tried first to preach "for all parties." However, he finally felt he had to terminate this tortuous dilemma and take a stand. For him, it was ironic that he now found himself having to oppose the historic institution he had himself originated. Two major considerations were vital in his mind: first, he had a sense of solidarity with his brother seafarers on the Thames. He knew from experience that seafarers often had to be "sought out"—in order to "carry religion on board to them." Also, he had a compelling vision of the vocation of the Bethel Flag on a global scale. The Port Society had so far not allowed the use of the Bethel Flag on the *Ark*; their very name—the Port of London Society—reflected a self-imposed restriction on outreach.

Aware that the situation called for more than mere "moral support," Smith saw it was time to turn to his "now opulent and influential connections." In true Nelson tradition, the former man-of-war's man resolved to "throw himself in the breach at whatever risk," and launch a new seafarers' mission society. The Bethel Movement was born for greater things and George Charles Smith was not the man to let it die in infancy.

CHAPTER 9
THE BETHEL FLAG GOES GLOBAL
(1819–1826)

Having once arrived at his decision—to free the Bethel emblem for its global destiny—George Charles Smith took on the task with typical vigor. First, he called a consultative meeting with brother seafarers on board a ship in the Upper Pool. They approved Smith's proposal to form a new society and to name it "The Bethel Seamen's Union" (BSU). With the Bethel banner as rallying point, they dedicated themselves to fellowship with one another and outreach to others everywhere.

Incidentally, it is a fact of history easily overlooked that this first "seafarers' union" ever created was not founded for sociopolitical purposes, which would have been banned by the prevailing Combination Acts. It was formed for the spiritual and overall welfare of fellow seafarers in Britain and worldwide.

With his decision now endorsed by his peers, Smith wrote two tracts in the fall of 1819 which both became widely read: *Bethel or the Flag Unfurled*; and *English Sailors* or *Britain's Best Bulwarks*. Together, the two publications traced the course of events leading up to the official founding of the Bethel Seamen's Union—an event that took place on November 12, 1819 at the City of London Tavern.

On behalf of what would now become the world's first national society for seafarers' mission, Smith was able to give his marketing skills free rein. He brought together inspiring speeches by a long list of naval officers, merchants, clergy, captains, and mates. Then, for his own part, he recalled how, as a sailor, he had witnessed the "grand triumphal entry of Lord Nelson and his Fleet into Kioge Bay in the Baltic, after the Battle of

Copenhagen. But ah! Nelson," he went on, "what were thy honours, and what were all thy glories, compared with this peaceful assembly—these bloodless [Bethel] banners—and this glorious Union to gather together in one the Seamen of my Country, and conduct them to honours and glories imperishable and durable as eternity!"

The nature of the new society would be somewhat reminiscent of the threefold pattern the Apostle Paul follows in Galatians 3:28: *global* in ethnicity—limited only by "the circumference of the Globe," *universal* in social status, and *ecumenical* in church affiliation, with "nothing whatever to do with religious denominations."

To further these purposes, the society would rely on four principal means: the Bethel Flag—as rallying point for gospel ministry among seafarers, not only at sea but also ashore; literary media—Scripture or tracts, including *The Sailor's Magazine*; foreign correspondence—to stimulate and coordinate similar work overseas; and other means—including "suitable boarding-houses for Sailors."

Thomas Thompson, now a respected Congregationalist, had—as Reverend John Newton's "pulpit boy"—learnt shorthand. In that way he would not have to miss a word when taking sermon notes as he listened to his idol. Ever since Smith's Scilly Islands Mission, Thompson had also been an eloquent supporter of Smith's projects. From the outset he served as an honorary secretary of the Port of London Society. At the founding of the Bethel Seamen's Union he publicly declared that supplementation and not competition now mandated a second metropolitan seafarers' mission society, with both institutions working "hand in hand" in each of their spheres.

Smith followed up on this idea by proposing to R. H. Marten, the new honorary treasurer of the Port of London Society, that this "Bethel Union," as it was called, could become an "auxiliary" of the PLS. However, the Port of London Society "politely declined" the offer. In fact, the latter even went so far as to "apprize the public" through the press that the new society did not in any way "emanate" from the Port of London Society, but would be quite "distinct" from this.

Smith would later see the founding of the Bethel Seamen's Union in 1819 as the original reason for the "open warfare" that erupted in 1827 between metropolitan-based seafarers' mission societies. That struggle proved to be one of principles, not personalities. People like Thomas Thompson and Thomas Phillips would later confirm that, together with Smith, they saw efforts by the PLS to restrain revivalism and lay collaboration as the root problem from the very start.

The Seamen's Preacher was now prepared to do battle—whatever the cost. If others saw the founding of the Bethel Seamen's Union as "a schism or secession," the BSU founders saw it as saving the Bethel Flag and all it stood for. They felt this conviction confirmed every time they saw the flag unfurling over new horizons. For them it was a symbol of expanding metropolitan efforts and promising beginnings elsewhere—not only in provincial but also foreign ports. In fact, in the years following 1819, the story of the *Seamen's Cause* would virtually become the story of the *Bethel Cause*—from the Thames River in London to the Pearl River in Canton.

Through both his speeches and his authorship, Smith played a key role in the publicizing of the Bethel Flag. As a result, the hoisting of the flag—for prayer meetings and preaching on shipboard—frequently led to the opening of a Bethel loft ashore or to the refitting of an old hulk as a floating chapel in the docks. By 1822, this had already led to the founding of a local Bethel Union or Seamen's Friend Society in five major UK port cities—Greenock, Leith, Bristol, Liverpool, and Hull.

In northeastern England, Smith maintained particularly close relations with the Port of Hull Society, where up to five thousand would crowd onto the floating chapel, as well as on adjacent ships and on shore, to listen to his powerful voice. As for the northwest, when Smith held a series of open-air shipboard sermons in Liverpool's docklands, seafarers filled the rigging of every ship in the vicinity. At a rally afterwards, so many responded by forming flag-carrying "Bethel Companies" that a local church leader turned to Smith and exclaimed: "This is going to heaven too fast!"

THE

SAILOR'S MAGAZINE,

AND

Naval Miscellany.

PUBLISHED UNDER THE PATRONAGE

OF THE

BRITISH AND FOREIGN

SEAMEN'S FRIEND SOCIETY,

AND

Bethel Union.

"The abundance of the sea shall be converted to Thee."

VOL. I.

LONDON:

Printed by T. Hamblin, Garlick Hill;

Published by W. SIMPKIN and R. MARSHALL, Stationers' Court, Ludgate-Street:

And sold by Whittemore, Paternoster Row; Robins, Tooley-street; Rubidge, ditto; Van, ditto; Delahoy, Deptford; Richardson, Greenwich; Hardcastle, Woolwich; Richardson, Bristol; Clark, St. Michael's Hill, Bristol; Kaye, Liverpool; Harris, Duke-street, Dock; Dodd's, South Shields; and all Booksellers in the Ports of Great Britain.

1820.

The world's first Maritime Mission magazine, launched by Smith in 1820, while still a pastor in Penzance and edited by him under various titles until he died in 1863.

From 1822, many new Bethel-affiliated societies began an ongoing relationship to the London-based "parent" society. The latter had, since 1820, expanded its name to the "British and Foreign Seamen's Friend

Society and Bethel Union" (BFSFSBU), with George Charles Smith as foreign secretary and magazine editor. By the mid-1820s, this unwieldy yet vibrant "Bethel Movement" had managed to proliferate around the entire coast of the British Isles, from the Shetland Islands in the north to the Channel Islands in the south.

The prefix "Foreign" in the designation "British and Foreign Seamen's Friend Society and Bethel Union" expressed the global dimension of the society—with the Bethel Flag as its symbol. In the global growth of the Bethel Movement, it was again Smith who played the central role, through his personal correspondence and his copious coverage through *The Sailor's Magazine*. He was also an ardent supporter of "schooling" foreign-bound clergy and missionaries in the Bethel system through prior attendance at live Bethel Meetings on the Thames. This is how preaching under the Bethel Flag was first established in North America.

As for Canada, Reverend Scott from Lyme, Dorsetshire, was planning to leave as an immigrant for St. John, New Brunswick, when he experienced the excitement of seafarers responding to Bethel preaching on the Thames. He declared he had "never witnessed such a scene in his life," and stated his "determination to establish similar meetings" on his arrival in Canada.

When Scott was about to embark from Devonport, Smith found the man had no Bethel Flag of his own. He promptly offered him the one he had just used himself at a crowded shipboard service. Scott was later reported to have put it to good purpose, gathering "great numbers" as he preached under the flag in the harbor of St. John.

Regarding the United States, in early 1821 Smith suggested in a letter to the recently founded New York Port Society that they should start an *American Sailor's Magazine*. He also "most forcibly" recommended the early adoption of the Bethel Flag as "a simple and cheap means" of enhancing the work. At the same time, a flag was given to Reverend John Allan, a visiting American Presbyterian minister who, before returning home, had also been amazed by the Bethel Meetings on the Thames. Nine days out of Liverpool, on March 11, 1821, Allan gazed with delight as he watched "the first Bethel Flag of the United States" flying from the masthead, while he conducted public worship on the New York packet *James Monroe.*

Within three months, a "New York Bethel Union" had been formed. Smith continued to urge his transatlantic colleagues to forge ahead with the Bethel Flag, a signal which he predicted would soon be "as well understood by sailors in every port of the world as a bell in every parish." In 1826, the Bethel Flag was officially adopted by the new American Seamen's Friend Society. It became a staple of new seafarers' mission societies all along the Atlantic coast. And by the end of the decade the flag was flying in a global network of American maritime mission endeavors—from the South Seas to Asia and on to South America.

Due to budgetary constraints and growing tensions between the BFSFSBU and the PLS, British-sponsored Bethel expansion was far less dramatic than that of America. Nevertheless, the BFSFSBU did supply captains, merchants, and especially foreign missionaries with Bethel Flags, tracts, and copies of *The Sailor's Magazine* for use in their respective seaports overseas.

Smith's most engaged colleague at the time was Reverend (former Captain) William Henry Angas. A one-time prisoner of war under Napoleon, Angas was the first to be ordained as a "Missionary to Seafaring Men" in 1821—in affiliation with the BFSFSBU. Not satisfied with Bethel beginnings only in British port cities, Angas determined "to push on to those ports where the message of love and mercy had not yet reached." In 1822, hoisting the Bethel Flag wherever he went, Angas took a tour of major continental port cities like Danzig, Hamburg, Rotterdam, and Antwerp.

Cut off by cholera at fifty-one, the short life of William Henry Angas nonetheless validated George Charles Smith's basic contention as to the primary aim of the Bethel Movement: "Every Christian on the seven seas must become what none other can be with equal effectiveness—a missionary among fellow seafarers!"

Another of Smith's Bethel colleagues was Danish-born Carl Gustav Christopher Ditlev von Bülow, a former cavalry officer who "enlisted in the army of the Lord" and became ordained as a Congregational minister. He, too, worked with the BFSFSBU. In his own specially built sailing chapel—with the Bethel Flag flying aloft—he set off to carry the gospel to the seafaring communities of Scandinavia. From 1819 to 1828, he made three major expeditions to Norway's coast-lands. Among local inhabitants he met with an overwhelming, positive response. However, he was finally forced to leave due to the negative reaction of Lutheran state church officials.

There were others, too, specifically a growing number of "Bethel Captains"—often veterans of the Thames Revival—who successfully pioneered Bethel meetings for the BFSFSBU. This occurred especially in Scandinavian, Russian, and Prussian port cities during the early 1820s. Smith witnessed with joy how the Bethel emblem now began fulfilling its global potential, as he always dreamed it would. One foreign sailor spoke for many of his peers when he exclaimed after a service under the Bethel Flag: "Good God, bless the Englishman—the sailor's best friend!"

CHAPTER 10
THE SAILOR'S "SODOM AND GOMORRAH"
(1819-1826)

"But we have a flag . . . " With those five words the editor of *The Sailor's Magazine* summarized the difference, between the modest assets of the Bethel Union Society in comparison with those of the Port of London Society and their Floating Chapel. George Charles Smith was happy to elaborate on the Bethel banner's call to seafarers and their friends to unite in "personal exertions throughout the world." The secret of the Bethel Movement's success was, more than anything, its simplicity. It was both economic and flexible—two vital factors for rapid expansion. With a few pieces of blue and white bunting and a convenient ship or an available room ashore, a seafarers' chapel could be "rigged" no matter where, with infinite possibilities.

However, Smith was also painfully aware that his pastorate was still in Penzance, far away from the London scene. His ministry there was still supposed to be his main source of income, as he battled with the bills of a fast-growing family. His rousing rhetoric had resulted in an enlargement of the Octagon Chapel in 1818, and again in 1822, when it was renamed the "Jordan Chapel." Repaying the resulting debts remained a constant challenge. Greater still was Smith's frustration from feeling that he somehow "belonged" on the front line of the struggle in the middle of London's Sailortown.

For Smith, it all seemed like a vicious circle. As he sought to reach a wider support base through his magazine, tracts, and travels, time for his own home and family decreased. In addition to his regular chapel trips to London every fall, speaking opportunities continued coming in from all around the country. One day, he would be off to a rally in Hull. Another day, he would be headed to Minehead and Watchet in the Bristol Channel to explain and defend the Bethel Flag. (Customs officials had been bullying Bethel pioneers on behalf of ship owners who were unhappy about mission work on board their vessels.)

Under constant financial pressure, Smith also tended to be querulous with members of the local clergy in Penzance who criticized his endless projects and blunt behavior. This came to a head in 1824 in the so-called Tuck-Net Controversy. The feud raged for several months, with sarcastic remarks about Smith as the "Bishop of the Baptists in Penzance," and unsubstantiated accusations of misappropriation of funds.

At the same time, Smith was keenly aware of the temptations to which sailors were constantly exposed in London. He was convinced that the crucial place from which to focus an effective counterstrategy would have to be "the very hub of London's maritime vice"—Sailortown. In the early 1820s, however, Smith had no intention of moving his home base from Penzance. Instead, he published plans to provide "pulpit supply" from time to time on the London waterfront, in cooperation with like-minded colleagues from elsewhere.

Smith gladly gave coverage, both in his magazine and in a tract called *The Press Gang*, to examples of evangelism among inhabitants in the heart of London's Sailortown. It began with the "Screw Bay Mission," started by sailors who had taken part in the services at Rotherhithe Methodist Chapel as early as in 1817.

Screw Bay was notorious as "the worst neighborhood in Rotherhithe" and was deliberately "fixed on" by participants in the current Bethel Meetings as a suitable scene for their enterprise on the south side. Soliciting a different room there for prayers every Sunday evening, they first ran into determined opposition. Nonetheless, they persevered. Within two or three years they began to see the conversion of "depraved watermen and abandoned women" where only "shameless immorality" had previously prevailed.

Among those who were deeply involved in the Screw Bay venture was Zebedee Rogers, the Bethel Flag originator. From 1821, Rogers became the leader of an even more ambitious plan on the north side of the river. Until now, mission endeavors among sailors in the port of London had been centered mainly among the collier shipping in the Pool of the Thames. However, much of the deep sea trade with East and West India was concentrated further east, on the north side. And "many a thought-less sailor, allured to the snares of sin," would continue to crowd through Stepney, which lay astride their main thoroughfare westward. It was here that Rogers and his Bethel friends from the river decided to raise their standard in a very literal sense.

The house Zebedee Rogers used in Stepney was essentially "a large coal shed." The shoemaker managed to fit up these primitive quarters as a relatively spacious meeting place. Here, with the aid of "a few pious Sail-ors," he began a Sunday evening religious meeting "for the good of the inhabitants" of the area. This was the beginning of the "Stepney Mission." Here a formerly "wicked waterman," now recently converted, spontane-ously exclaimed: "O Lord! We have heard thou hast blessed the hoisting of the Bethel Flag from ship to ship. Oh Lord, I pray thee, bless it from house to house!"

The plan adopted by the Sailortown team was simple and effective. For most of the week, Zebedee Rogers kept busy, leading prayer meet-ings in the Lower Pool. Then, toward the end of the week, he would call for volunteers to the "Bethel Meeting House," as his former coal shed came to be called. Here, a group of resolute tars would meet early Sunday morning for prayers and a brief breakfast. After this, they would scatter for a round of neighborhood visits, focusing first on residents. They would knock on doors, offer tracts to people who "scarcely ever entered the House of God," and then invite them to the evening "Sailors' Meeting" there in Stepney.

For the rest of the day, Rogers and his partners would concern them-selves principally with sailors. Hailing their unsuspecting colleagues in streets and fields, or hunting them up in boarding houses and brothels, they countered scoffing and swearing with cheerful rejoinders in nauti-cal jargon. They just kept pushing and pulling, well aware that none were "more capable of attracting the notice of seamen than seamen themselves."

Wherever there was a sermon in a nearby chapel advertised as "profess-edly to sailors," they would bring along a motley band of mariners. A final foray on the way back would climax the day with a crowded evening meeting at Stepney's Bethel Mission House. Soon there was also a need for Wednesday evening meetings.

The "Sea Missionaries," were both enthusiastic and resourceful. For example, a "gentleman of the neighbourhood" happened to stop a seafarer who was eagerly leading a fellow mariner along to the evening's meeting. He reminded the sailor that this was a free country and that, since the war was over and men were no longer wanted for the navy, no man could be "forced anywhere against his will." He demanded to know what the sailor meant to do with such men. The reply was to the point: "Sir, there is an everlasting war proclaimed against the kingdom of darkness, and we are on the impress service for the king of kings."

The surprised questioner found he could only wish God's blessings upon such a novel yet noble endeavor. When a constable, using abusive language, demanded an explanation on a similar occasion, he was effec-tively silenced by a tract called *The Swearer's Prayer*, pressed deftly into his hand by one of the band of Sea Missionaries.

As for seafarers themselves, those who had been hauled into "Sailors' Meetings" from neighboring "dens of iniquity" were shocked to discover many of their brother sailors praying fervently. When the landlord of a large public house in Wapping (The Royal Oak) agreed to let the Stepney Mission use his premises for religious meetings on Sundays, this proved a great help in their outreach. An enterprising "press gang" from the mis-sion made the most of this by flying the Bethel Flag from oars they stuck through the pub's windows "fore and aft."

It did not take long before the building was filled with both sailors and landsfolk from the neighborhood. This unlikely "congregation" would then discover a very different kind of meeting than they had anticipated in a public house. Nonetheless, no one would normally leave before the close.

Friends of the Bethel cause decided that Zebedee Rogers' work was so important that it needed to be more structured. At a public meeting on September 28, 1821 they organized the "Stepney and Wapping Bethel Mission Society," with George Charles Smith in the chair. Smith secured the election of Zebedee Rogers as secretary, Thomas Phillips as treasurer, and six pioneer Bethel captains as committee members.

Unfortunately, Rogers' strenuous efforts took their toll on both his health and his relationships. This eventually forced him to leave his leadership to others. Smith stood by his friend to the end. When Rogers died in 1833, he was serving as superintendent of a Stepney-based shelter for destitute sailors, founded by Smith and called "The Sailors' Rest." After the funeral—in what was now London's Mariners' Church—Smith wrote how this one-time shoemaker and devoted originator of the Bethel emblem had been "buried with all the Bethel flags and honours that grateful hearts could procure, amidst a host of spectators."

Meanwhile, back in 1824, Smith was becoming more convinced than ever of the need for a "Second Metropolitan Marine Establishment." If London was to exercise leadership worthy of its maritime significance, there was no way this could be achieved with the limited resources of only one Port Society and its floating chapel. While the Stepney Mission struggled on ashore, Smith focused on a "New Floating Chapel"—also on the north side of the river, but closer to the Tower than that of the Port Society.

Disputing a public statement by the PLS that "at present no new facility was required beyond their own," Smith provided the BFSFSBU with statistical evidence to the contrary. Still, plans for a Bethel-linked floating chapel on the north side were voluntarily put on hold—in deference to a group of Anglican churchmen. In response to constant preaching and encouragement by Smith and his friends, it now seemed likely that an "Episcopal Floating Church" for the Thames would soon be opened in exactly that area. No one then knew it would still take another five years before this would happen.

In the meantime, Smith returned to the concept of a shore-based facility. This finally began to take shape in 1825. The year before, he had come across the old, disused Danish-Norwegian Church in Wellclose Square. He had discovered it during one of his north bank Sailortown field surveys. He recommended it to the committee of the BFSFSBU before leaving London for the winter. On his return in the summer of 1825, he was exasperated to find that nothing had been done. Facing the collapse of the whole project, he made the momentous decision to act independently.

Smith began with a series of Sabbath morning open-air services on Tower Hill. Huge crowds gathered while he repeatedly "pressed upon their attention" the need for a "Mariners' Church" near the London Dock Gates. The campaign culminated with a meeting in August where "at least 5,000 souls" heard the Sailors' Preacher make his pitch—for a building where mariners might at last be "arrested in their fatal career to destruction" by all the "hardened plunderers of their property."

Before the end of August, Smith had contracted with the trustees of the Danish-Norwegian Church to rent their building for £50 per year, after needful repairs. He also collected "a few friends" into a provisional committee. Then, at a public meeting at the City of London Tavern, a "Mariners' Church Society" was founded on September 6, 1825. While introducing themselves as a distinct institution, the MCS announced that they nevertheless wished to be considered a "Branch Society" of the BFSFSBU. At the same time, by adopting the term "Mariners' Church" they were deliberately imitating a usage already familiar in the United States.

Smith wrote about the new venture as particularly promising "because it came spontaneously from a British Sailor's heart." Hearing of the intended Mariners' Church at the close of one of Smith's open-air services, a passing tar had reportedly called out: "Clear the gangway there, I've got a shot in the locker yet. I'll help anything that does good to poor Jack. Here, shipmate, here's my sixpence to begin with." Later, Smith's faithful friend, Thomas Thompson, forwarded fifty guineas to him, together with words of encouragement to not give up. That settled it. In December 1825, repairs were ready and Britain's first, shore-based "Mariners' Church" was opened to the public.

Such were both the building and its location that Smith would speak warmly about them both for years to come, seeing it all as "a sort of divine arrangement." The building itself was certainly well suited to its new purpose, steeped as it was in maritime tradition. Completed in 1696, this impressive "Templum Dano-Norvegicum" had since then served as the Lutheran place of worship in London for both resident and seafaring Danes and Norwegians. With the dissolution of the union between these two countries in 1814, the congregation, too, disintegrated. Nevertheless, the structure was still seen as sound and capable of holding about one thousand people.

The site of the church, at the center of the green in Wellclose Square, could hardly have been more strategic. Formerly known as "Marine Square"—due to the many merchants, ship owners and captains living there at the time—the neighborhood had recently undergone a great deal of change. After the construction of the London Docks southeast of the Square—with St. Katherine's Docks soon to follow southwest of it—these quarters had now been taken over by the poverty-ridden families of seafarers and waterfront workers. Leading up to the Square was notorious Ratcliffe Highway. And surrounding it was a network of such ill repute that the area was now considered the very core of Sailortown depravity.

Here, crowds of seafarers would converge regularly from as far afield as Limehouse and Blackwall. Wellclose Square was where "Boatswain Smith" now determined to raise the Bethel emblem. And he certainly made no secret of his ultimate goal—to transform what he saw as London's "Sodom and Gomorrah of Sailors" into a modern-day "Marine Jerusalem."

CHAPTER 11
TOWARD A "MARINE JERUSALEM"
(1826-1829)

In his quest to create a "Marine Jerusalem" among the brothels and sailors' saloons surrounding Wellclose Square, Smith could not escape the personal cost such a transformation would entail. After his 1824 field study of the shadowy haunts of Wapping, he wrote in *The Sailor's Magazine*: "No good will ever be done to the mass of Sailors in London until we have settled amongst them, like missionaries amongst the heathen. One must be *amongst the Sailors* to be affected with their miseries."

For his part, Smith realized this would demand his all. He knew not least that it might have negative consequences for his family—until then living in the relative peace of a picturesque Penzance. Despite his voluminous writings, with eventually some eighty publications to his name, Smith made little mention of his family in them. However, from the scattered sources available, it is clear that they were not immune from the storms and stresses of the public life of the family head.

By 1824, Smith's family was already numerous. It was in June 1808 at Blackfriars, London, that Smith married Theodosia, a daughter of the Yorkshire Baptists, John and Rebecca Skipworth; Theodosia was born at Earl's Court, Brompton. After joining her husband in Penzance, records reveal she bore him ten children while living there—six sons and four daughters.

The family's first home was in Chapel Street, later moving to the Jordan Chapel's parsonage at Regent Terrace. As already noted, Smith's young wife voiced angry protests early in their marriage, when her husband's postage debts reached an "unbearable" level as a result of the rapid growth of his Naval Correspondence Mission. Though he managed to obtain temporary help from a number of supporters at the time, financial problems would continue to plague Smith and his family throughout his long career.

When Smith headed home again from London in March 1826, he hesitated at first to make the actual move from Penzance. Nonetheless, he records that he felt he had no choice but to "yield up" both his church and salary there. With "no prospect of a penny" beyond what he might bring in himself, he finally transferred himself and his family from his parsonage in Penzance to the center of London's Sailortown—at No. 19 Wellclose Square. In so doing, he would soon find it meant saying farewell to more than two decades of relative security at his home on the Cornish coast.

With Smith now literally in their midst, as the first full-time seafarers' minister in the nation, it placed the committee of the BFSFSBU in a difficult situation. In order to finance the many ministries Smith had in mind for the new Mariners' Church, he would have to build up nationwide support. When the BFSFSBU did not accept Smith's offer of cooperation in the use of the new building, he reluctantly resigned his position as their secretary. In response, the committee sent Smith, who was, after all, their founder figure, a resolution of good wishes for success in his "new sphere of action."

Meanwhile, Smith was still the editor of *The Sailor's Magazine*. The committee of the BFSFSBU, under whose patronage the magazine had existed since 1820, was well aware of Smith's exceptional qualifications for this task and was anxious to avoid a rival publication. However, when a compromise the committee suggested proved "too restrictive" for Smith and his new society, the BFSFSBU "discontinued" Smith's editorial services from January 1827. As the magazine's originator, Smith found this action hard to swallow and at once started a successor called *The New Sailor's Magazine*.

These two tangible "assets," the London Mariners' Church and *The New Sailor's Magazine*, would continue to be the dual mainstays in "Boatswain Smith's" stormy life. Come what may, he managed somehow to hang on to both for many years, the church—until he was finally evicted in 1845, and the magazine—until he died in 1863.

In hindsight, it was Smith's action in August 1825, renting the Danish-Norwegian Church in Wellclose Square, which set in motion a chain of events creating such a deep rupture between Britain's metropolitan seafarers' mission societies. Before addressing the tumultuous times ahead, it is relevant to look at the shape of the "Marine Jerusalem" that Smith originally envisioned.

On the first anniversary of the BFSFSBU in 1820, Smith had addressed the chairman, Lord Gambier, with the following assertion: "There is, my Lord, one favourite motto of mine—*Go forward!*" For Smith's restless personality, this was a categorical imperative. Once convinced of a course of action, he could not remain passive. This applied also to the *Seamen's Cause*. Given the success of the Bethel Movement elsewhere, Smith reasoned, why was the great marine metropolis of London lagging so far behind?

He noted that the annual income of the parent Bethel Union had never exceeded £500. To the publicity-minded Smith, the vicious circle of "the low state of things in London" could only be broken by demonstrating to the public "a tangible source of expenditure." Such a source, Smith believed, was precisely what the new "Metropolitan Marine Establishment" in Wellclose Square represented.

With that, Smith set to—after first hoisting a large Bethel Flag from the roof of the London Mariners' Church. Here, he would try to implement the "Sailor Emancipation" for which he had agitated since 1823. Smith saw the oppression of his fellow seafarers as twofold: The first consisted of physical and economic distress connected with the very nature of the seafarer's vocation, such as shipwreck or enemy action. The second was linked to human causes, summed up in the form of Sailortown extortion defined above as the so-called Crimping System.

In Penzance, Smith had often given examples of his comprehensive approach to maritime outreach. He believed that spiritual and physical welfare were inseparably linked. Given the explosive growth of the Bethel Movement in the early 1820s, seafarers could no longer say that no one cared about their souls. How tragic indeed, Smith declared, if seafarers should now have to ask: "Why do you attend to our souls and neglect our bodies?"

In 1824, Smith took part in the founding of the Royal National Institution for the Preservation of Life from Shipwreck (today known as the Royal National Life-boat Institution). Later that year, he succeeded in including seafarers' bereaved dependents in a Shipwrecked and Distressed Sailors' Family Fund, in affiliation with the BFSFSBU (now called the Shipwrecked Fishermen and Mariners' Royal Benevolent Society).

Aid for the needy did not necessarily take the form of monetary support. In the late 1820s, Smith organized a Destitute Sailors' Clothing Department at his headquarters in Wellclose Square. To provide practical help for this endeavor, Smith started several Ladies' Maritime Associations during his travels, enlisting a number of "ladies of nobility" for the cause. At the same time, he organized local "pious females" to form a Mariners' Infant Friend Society. These were intended to "visit and relieve, by a small donation and the loan of a box of useful Linen, the distressed Sailor's wife during the months of her confinement."

Smith had only just settled down with his family in Wellclose Square on New Year's Eve when he had to confront the immediate need for another form of social action. It was "a cold frosty night, with hail and sleet." A large number of destitute sailors had found their way from surrounding streets and taken part in a watch night service at the Mariners' Church. Smith recalls how it was past two in the morning when they lined up along the sidewalk by the church doors:

> As I walked to the gates, they sighed, and cried most piteously that they had no shelter, no food, no clothes but the rags about them. I was filled with horror, to think that I and members [of the church] had comfortable rooms and fires and beds, but these poor sailors, unto whom we owed all, were left to perish. Therefore, I resolved to have a shelter provided, and, if possible, a biscuit and basin of plain soup in the morning, and another in the evening, and then out in the day to look for a ship that wanted men, and that there should be preaching to them every evening.

Within a week, Smith's vision had begun to take shape in nearby Dock Street as the nation's first Destitute Sailors' Asylum. Dock Street was described as "a dirty narrow lane," running parallel to the west side of Wellclose Square. Amidst the many brothels located there, Smith discovered an old deserted warehouse which offered a possible alternative. Although bereft of funds as usual, he promptly rented the building.

Smith was soon joined by two retired naval officers, George Gambier and Robert Elliott. They had heard of Smith's efforts and wanted to help. They even offered to take financial responsibility for the venture. First, the lower floor was fitted as a mess room for serving a staple diet of soup. Then the loft was covered with straw for sleeping quarters. On January 8, 1828, the building could be officially opened.

Nonetheless, as another winter set in, many more shivering sailors— often shoeless, even shirtless—continued to make their way to the Mariners' Church and Smith's "Mariners' House" at No. 19. The Square had by now become known as a sort of "Metropolitan Mecca" for maritime welfare. Smith was not the man to betray his fellow seafarers' trust and went ahead to secure a sorely needed supplementary shelter. Near Cannon Street Road he finally succeeded to obtain a Shipwrecked and Distressed Sailors' Asylum. Opened in 1830, it was taken over by the Anglicans two years later.

"Boatswain Smith" was aware that cases of "maritime distress" might well be linked to external causes such as shipwreck, enemy action, unemployment, disease, or advanced age. However, a major reason for the ruin of many lives was the sailors' own "proneness to the vices of the lower orders," such as "drunkenness and debauchery." Still, Smith would not accept social bias. As he put it: "We are not set to judge of evil actions, but to relieve distress. Reject men under any circumstances at the Asylum, and we see little hope for them but to live by begging, or to die of starvation; receive them, and we know not a condition of misery and evil from which, by the blessing of God, they may not be reclaimed."

Despite efforts to provide for better material relief and spiritual care for sailors and their dependents, Smith knew that no solution would be possible without coming to grips with the root causes of their plight. He therefore went in for expansive plans for systemic reform. He was unable to implement most of them himself. But Smith deserves credit for being the first to focus public attention on the social realities of that "universal system of maritime plunder" known as the Crimping System. He also supplied a comprehensive strategy for its elimination.

By the 1820s, the "crimp" was already well established, on the British waterfront as elsewhere in the maritime world. From its original meaning of "forcing to comply"—often fraudulently—the term "crimping" had, by the 1800s, come to designate the luring of sailors to enlist in departing ships. All persons engaged in directing this practice were collectively referred to as "crimps."

In practice, the crimp's goal was simply to separate the sailor from his hard-earned wages, whether by fair means or foul—usually foul. To reduce sailors to the desired level of compliance, a successful crimp would enlist a whole hierarchy of helpers. Key people among them would be bar owners and boardinghouse keepers. At the same time, the crimp would work with any or all of the following fellow workers: "runners" (who would make contact with crews aboard newly arrived ships), "brothel-keepers," "pot-house bullies," "cheating slop-sellers," and "pettyfogging sea-lawyers."

With the aid of such helpers, the crimp would meet the two most basic needs of any homecoming sailor: relief—from the hardships and stress of sea-life, and reemployment—when no longer willing or able to remain ashore. By a system of "marine slavery"—as Smith called it—the sailor was first stripped of whatever he had earned on his arrival in port, then of any wage advance obtainable on his departure. Incredibly enough, this unscrupulous behavior had long since established itself as the principal form of shipping agency of the day. (In England it was not till 1915 that the practice was finally forbidden by law.)

In his anti-crimping campaign, "Boatswain Smith" refused to compromise, as many of his time did. Having once "sighted the enemy," he was relentless in his pursuit. While still a pastor at Penzance, he published dramatic exposés of this whole system of condoned extortion. He showed how naval seafarers, too, were enticed into the clutches of the crimp. Later, in London, he alleged that the voracious land sharks there were "a thousand times worse than sharks at sea." (A sailor might at least be fortunate enough to avoid the latter!)

After moving to Wellclose Square in 1926, Smith intensified his anti-crimping tactics to a system of substitution. Any "service" rendered by a crimp had to be met with positive alternatives at every turn. One universal need for deep-sea sailors was boarding and lodging facilities between voyages. This fact was the stronghold of the Crimping System. It was therefore the logical place to start the competition.

In ports like Liverpool, Leith, Greenock, and Bristol, efforts had been made by the local seafarers' ministry to set up a plan for "recommended" boarding houses. By this means, the crimp's monopoly had to some extent been broken. But it was by no means eliminated—least of all in London, where strife between seafarers' mission societies during the 1820s had unfortunately left the crimp relatively undisturbed.

As forlorn seafarers clamored daily for admittance to the recently opened Destitute Sailors' Asylum in Dock Street, Smith was acutely aware that their numbers would simply continue to swell—unless they were met with an alternative before they were enmeshed in the "crimping net." Then, like a bolt from the blue, came the sensational collapse of the newly built Brunswick Theatre the morning of February 28, 1828. Despite all the human tragedy which he, too, deeply deplored, Smith wrote that he saw this as a manifestation of not only divine judgment but also providence. Certainly, the consequences for the *Seamen's Cause* would be far-reaching.

The Brunswick Theatre had been raised on the site of the old Royalty Theatre in Well Street, between Dock Street and Wellclose Square. Before the Royalty's destruction by fire in 1826, this theater had, for a long time, gained notoriety as a focal point for crimps, thieves and "harlots." As a result, the place had—according to Smith—caused ruin for thousands of gullible tars. Then, that fateful February morning in 1828, Smith was alerted by one of his agents, thundering at his door and shouting that the new Brunswick theater had just collapsed. From that moment, Smith reacted with a resolution worthy of one of Nelson's men.

A rehearsal had been in progress when, without warning, the roof caved in and scores were buried in the rubble. At once, Smith sent for every available man at the nearby Destitute Sailors' Asylum. For the next nine hours, he supervised the work of digging out the dead and wounded. Then, standing amid the ruins, he had a vision. Only shortly before, he had published the desperate need, as he saw it, for some large "Sailors' Depot" with facilities for receiving and reshipping discharged—as opposed to destitute—seafarers. Was not God now pointing out the place? Perhaps God would turn the disasters of both 1826 and now 1828 to something good.

The ruins of the Royal Brunswick Theatre in Well Street, London, the scene of Smith's rescue campaign just after the roof caved in on February 28, 1828. (Courtesy of The Sailors' Society)

The place had once been the site of a chapel. What could be more appropriate, reasoned Smith, than to "restore" the ground to God for the rescue, instead of the ruin, of seafarers? With all the "determination of his soul," Smith sallied forth to achieve exactly that. He preached to vast crowds of incredulous sightseers, with thousands of hearers at a time. He also rushed off a series of six tracts about the tragedy.

On September 10, 1828, to the "astonishment and horror" of crimps among the onlookers, Smith held a historic public meeting on the site, marking an agreement for leasehold of the ground and solemnly dedicating it to its new purpose. Then, on January 8, 1829, again on Smith's initiative, the "Sailors' Home," or "Royal Brunswick Maritime Establishment," was officially founded at the City of London Tavern. This marked the origin of the world's first multiservice "Sailors' Home," a term coined by Smith.

Among the first to volunteer their support were the naval captains George Gambier and Robert Elliott, both of whom were already involved with the Destitute Sailors' Asylum in Dock Street. These were again able to bring in many of their Anglican colleagues. Meanwhile, through his magazine, tracts, and speeches, Smith elaborated on his "Sailors' Home Plan," as the society's honorary secretary. At first the plan seemed quite drastic:

(1) "A Receiving and Shipping Depot"—seen as the major ministry of the new facility. Here, on the invitation of agents a sailor could, at a reasonable rate, find safety, board, and lodging; also a museum, library, saving bank, and (even more disastrous for the Crimping System) a "Seamen's Register Office," based on service and character references.

(2) "A Sailors' Refuge"—for seafarers who, though not yet "destitute" to the point of "soup and straw," still needed a place to "hang a hammock and ride out a temporary storm."

(3) "A Sea Boys' Rendezvous,"—in order to provide pre-sea training for boys smitten with "sea-fever," or simply to stem the rising tide of juvenile delinquency.

Through all three of these services, the intention was to provide a common thread of "Christian discipline," "religious instruction," "domestic prayers," and "Sabbath observance." Despite the nondenominational basis for Smith's plan, most of it never materialized. A "sudden crisis" surfaced among the leaders of the venture, spurred by the current "Irvingite" controversy within the Anglican Communion. At its core was the Reverend Edward Irving, notorious for urgently underscoring Christ's imminent return. Among Irving's most ardent supporters was Captain George Gambier.

The practical George Charles Smith had little patience for such end-of-time speculations. He decided to withdraw from the original plan and instead launch a far more comprehensive project. In October 1829, he called a preliminary public meeting at the Mariners' Church, after publishing the prospectus for a "Sailors' Rest" or "Maritime Guardian Establishment." As he insisted, "No half measures will do to destroy the crimping system!" Beside the features he had already included in his three-point plan for the Well Street Sailors' Home, he was convinced that the seagoing sailor must have access to what he now designated "a total remedy." This new project would need to include the following further features:

(1) "Comprehensive Maritime Medical Care"—providing primarily a "Convalescent Haven" for those discharged from hospital but needing further recovery; also, a "Sailors' Infirmary" for assisting with continuing non-hospital afflictions; and finally a "Merchant Seamen's Hospital" for geriatric care, to give "peace and piety" to two thousand to three thousand "disabled and worn-out mariners." (This would go beyond the limited naval scope of the existing Greenwich Royal Hospital.) In close proximity to these facilities would be the establishment of what was believed to be the first "Sailors' Cemetery" in the world.

(2) "A Sailors' Anchorage"—comprising not only a place of temporary residence but also a "Sailors' Legal Aid" (to rescue sailors from unscrupulous "sea-lawyers"); a dependable "Sailors' Slop-chest" (to compete with the sub-standard articles of use offered by dishonest crimps); and finally, "Maritime Lectures" (on themes of special relevance).

The goal for Smith's maritime social action was, in keeping with current thinking, to have every merchant mariner pass through a kind of "moral hospital" before shipping out. Eventually, he wrote, this would result in a whole "new race of seamen."

Smith's hopes were abruptly dashed by the organizational meltdown which came to be seen as "the disaster of 1832." Meanwhile, a calmer time among the Anglicans gave Captain George Gambier's more moderate colleague, Captain Elliott Gambier, the chance to introduce a more acceptable society structure for at least part of Smith's plans.

With restored public confidence and renewed interest on the part of ship owners, work on what had for so long been the "carcass" of a building was resumed. Thanks to the determination of Captain Elliott Gambier, the Sailors' Home in Well Street was finally opened in May 1835. As a pioneer in its field, the institution met such a widely felt need that it was soon emulated by many others. For its own part, it lasted until 1974.

The world's first "Sailors' Home," conceived by Smith on the site of the ruined Royal Brunswick Theatre in Well Street, London and completed in 1835. (Courtesy of The Sailors' Society)

As early as in November 1829, Captain Elliott Gambier had, at a public meeting at the City of London Tavern, already recognized Smith's role as founder and principal promoter of the original Sailors' Home. As for Smith's plans for a wider-ranging "Sailor's Rest," he did at least identify legitimate needs in an age not yet prepared to recognize them. In fact, the Sailors' Pastor from Penzance had chartered a course in maritime social reform that future generations could not, in the long run, continue to ignore.

CHAPTER 12

TUMULTUOUS TIMES
(1829-1848)

Much as he would have loved to, George Charles Smith never managed to write an overall history of mission in the seafaring world. When the year 1829 led him into even more tumultuous times, he stated in his magazine four years later that any future historian would have to face a formidable task—"to sift and investigate for truth amidst the rubbish of reports, speeches, circulars, and resolutions" that had continued to surface on the London scene. Still, given the cost and course of the conflict that ensued, it seems important to attempt at least an outline of that time. This applies especially to a biography of the embattled founder of the Maritime Mission Movement that emerged around him.

The seeds of discord were sown as early as in 1819. It was a combined emphasis on revival and lay activism that led to the formation of the Bethel Union Society that year. Under the guiding hand of Smith, this grassroots movement had grown rapidly—despite the "foreboding shadows" he sensed among some within the Port of London Society. Prominent among the latter was Smith's one-time friend from the founding of that society the year before, Robert Humphrey Marten.

Marten had doubted the concept of lay-led Bethel Meetings from the start. Later, the PLS committee experienced a discouraging decline in the attendance at their floating chapel, together with a disheartening level of support. They also realized that their perceived isolationism had cost them that vital asset of any seafarers' ministry—the goodwill of seafarers themselves.

Meanwhile, the Bethel Union Society—now known as the British and Foreign Seamen's Friend Society and Bethel Union (BFSFSBU)—had recently also given evidence of being "in a declining state." With the founding of Smith's new Mariners' Church Society (MCS) in 1825, the BFSFSBU and PLS realized they were both faced with the prospect of a thriving third non-denominational "Seamen's Society" in the Metropolis. They finally found they would have more to gain by joining forces than by remaining apart.

The two societies came together officially at a public meeting in 1827, at the Argyle Rooms in Regent Street. Here, under the chair of Admiral Lord Gambier, they merged into the "Port of London and Bethel Union Society" (PLBUS), with the admiral as president. The union was sealed with the hoisting of the Bethel Flag for the first time on board the Floating Chapel.

Smith now felt free to rename his own organization (the MCS) as the "British and Foreign Seamen's and Soldiers' Friend Society" (BFSSFS). In reaction to this move, the PLBUS engaged Dr. John Styles, a Congregational minister known as a stirring and often controversial orator, as editor of *The Sailor's Magazine*—the position Smith had recently been forced to give up.

Styles at once launched into a personal attack on Smith, accusing him of instigating schism by "bearing our colours, but making war on our resources." Smith responded in kind with a whole series of tracts. One who had "stood the fire of the hottest battles" at sea was not "afraid of squibs and crackers" from shore. In that vein, Smith roundly rejected each of Styles' arguments.

Confronted with the continued success of Smith's society, in contrast to their own fast diminishing support, the committee of the PLBUS became alarmed. By early 1829, Dr. Styles had prepared a scathing 144-page denunciation entitled: *An Appeal to the Public, Being an answer to the Misrepresentation and Calumnies of the Rev. G. C. Smith*. As Smith himself saw it, the intent was nothing less than to "blast and destroy" his reputation all over the kingdom. The potentially harmful effect of the attack was nonetheless neutralized from a quite unexpected quarter.

Thomas Thompson and Thomas Phillips, both veterans of the *Seamen's Cause* from Thames Revival days, had served as honorary secretaries of the two societies that merged in 1827. These respected leaders caused a sensation when they resigned the following year, from both the Port Society and Bethel Union. Then, after failing in a final peace attempt, they published a forty-page pamphlet entitled, *Refutation: Being a Reply to the "Appeal" of the Port of London Society*.

The two men mentioned the inactivity and inflexibility of the PLBUS as their main reason for resigning. While not willing to exonerate Smith for being temperamental, they invalidated every charge of the *Appeal* against both his character and his integrity. Thompson added a prediction: "The records of history which shall tell of a Howard for prisoners and a Wilberforce and Clarkson for slaves, shall also tell of George Charles Smith as the unwearied, disinterested, faithful labourer for seamen of the world."

As a newcomer, Styles had exposed himself to both omissions and contradictions in his publication. Nor did his subsequent *Reply* change the effect of Thompson and Phillips' *Refutation*. By May 1829, the BFSSFS could show four times the income of the PLBUS, as well as a well-attended Mariners' Church. As for George Charles Smith himself, he experienced a peak of public respect in the summer of 1929, with no less than Admiral Lord Gambier heading the list of his naval patrons.

One of Smith's clergy supporters expressed the hope that his friend would soon have to fight with "no other foe than the prince of darkness." That hope was soon to be frustrated. After what proved to be only a brief respite, both Smith and the BFSSFS would be subjected to two very different forms of attack.

The first of these, the so-called Philo-Veritas Controversy, was a poison-pen campaign launched by a misinformed secretary of the PLBUS. His letters charged Smith with gross embezzlement, causing considerable commotion in both press and pulpit before they were exposed as totally unfounded. They were followed by the public apology of the author. (Smith's refusal to publish the name of his anonymous accuser was the only redeeming feature of the whole sorry affair.)

Next was the "Voice Controversy" in the summer of 1831. This was equally unsubstantiated but led to far more fateful consequences. In his hardworking crew, "Boatswain Smith" had no patience with "stowaways." In the spring of 1831, he had dismissed some he saw as "worthless servants," among them Joseph Mead, his recording secretary. In response to a charge of "excessive indolence," the relatively young Mead published a sixty-eight-page tract entitled, *A Voice from Wellclose Square.*

Mead's tract claimed fraudulent behavior by both Smith and his Society. Shortly afterwards, it was backed up with attacks from John Sibree, a leading Congregational minister in Coventry. Following this, a "confluence of discarded agents" joined in with anonymous letters and pamphlets. The combined effect of these onslaughts was to bring the Society to the brink of ruin.

Despite a debt fund, launched with the Lord Mayor of London himself as treasurer, it all escalated into a losing battle. Then, as creditors continued to clamor, Smith struck upon a plan which at first seemed to offer hope. The BFSSFS would institute a "public inquiry" into the affairs of the Society, to be carried out by an interdenominational committee of twenty well-known ministers and laymen. Such a committee did, in fact, conduct four days of exhaustive examination of facilities, staff, and accounts. In the report which they then published, Smith and his colleagues were "completely exonerated from any misappropriation or want of integrity."

While warmly commending Smith's general conduct of the Society and all its "highly adapted" activities, the report did make certain recommendations, among them the formation of a board of directors. By June 1832, a provisional board of "Metropolitan Dissenting Ministers" was formed, including Dr. Francis Augustus Cox, the Baptist minister of Hackney. To this group, Smith willingly transferred the entire management of the Society—with the exception of those two "non-negotiable" items, his Mariners' Church and his magazine.

Then, in August of the same year, the whole board abruptly announced their unanimous withdrawal. Smith's indignation knew no bounds. By their "desertion," the newly appointed directors had, as he put it, dealt a deliberate "deathblow" to "the greatest Seamen's Society in the kingdom."

It appeared later that the ministers had, in fact, tried to negotiate a "cordial union" between the PLBUS and the BFSSFS. These negotiations foundered, due to Smith's refusal to abandon any potential attempt to form an alternative organization. As for the embattled "Boatswain" himself, his compulsive sense of vocation gave him no choice: "I dare not leave the work," he said, "I should as soon think of drowning myself in the Thames. I am chained to the oar."

Smith announced that "to save the cause from the most fatal shipwreck and the most lubberly pilots," he welcomed fellow "blue jackets" to the launching of a new society at the City of London Tavern on October 10, 1832. The response appeared at first encouraging. So much so that, within half a year, the new society's receipts had exceeded those of its rival for a full year. From the following April, the Society adopted the title "British and Foreign Sailors' and Soldiers' Bethel Flag Union" (BFSSBFU).

Meanwhile, those who had tried to establish a single national seafarers' mission were not passive. Eventually, they succeeded in merging the PLBUS into a new organization, also founded at the City of London Tavern, on July 3, 1833, as the "British and Foreign Sailors' Society" (BFSS). Among those elected to the board of directors were "the most influential merchants and ministers in London."

By including the PLBUS—a successor to the original Port of London Society—the BFSS (or "Sailors' Society," as it is now called) could claim 1818 as its year of origin. In due course, the Society would also claim George Charles Smith as its earliest pioneer. However, by 1833, the continuing turmoil in London had resulted in two distinct nondenominational seafarers' mission organizations, both claiming to be national in scope: Smith's BFSSBFU and a strongly supported BFSS.

Despite the daunting problems Smith still faced, his new society not only survived, it even thrived. For the year 1833–1834, the BFSSBFU could publish an income level four times that of the BFSS. "I waited not for chapels," wrote Smith of these years, "but a fortnight every month went right through the country preaching anywhere and everywhere." Smith's imagination worked on overtime as he searched incessantly for new ways to promote the spiritual and social betterment of his fellow seafarers. His plans spanned from the more politicized to those directly involved with personal welfare, such as addiction issues.

In 1835, the crusade of Samuel Plimsoll to counter the most cynical neglect of safety at sea was still a generation ahead. However, Smith was at that time already protesting the use of "sea coffins, or frail ships, built cheap, to be lost to gain the insurance." Three years later, Smith's society was the first to found a religious organization specifically benefiting the new category of seafarers known as "steamers." To serve this "British and Foreign Steamers' Friend Society," Smith proposed a steam tug—called a "Steamers' Ark"—to commute from London Bridge to Gravesend. He was also involved in the emancipation of that abused class of Thames-side stevedores known as "coal-whippers."

In addition, Smith helped pave the way for important reforms to combat the brutal treatment of seafarers at sea—from impressment to arbitrary cruelty. During the Opium War of 1839–42, "Boatswain Smith" petitioned Queen Victoria about his country's shameful role in forcing that deadly drug onto the citizens of China. "How would God judge," he wrote, "Christian peoples who would permit poison to be thrust down the throats of a non-Christian nation at the point of the bayonet?" Worse yet, he added, was the fact that British sailors were made involuntary accessories to such crime.

Well before the collapse of Smith's organization in 1832, Smith had already been battling what he saw as the two constant enemies of the well-being of sailors—prostitution and drunkenness. Each of them was a key component of the crimping system. In both cases, Smith maintained a multi-faceted response throughout the 1830s.

In regard to prostitution, Smith was particularly merciless in his campaign against the condoned promiscuity he had witnessed during his own years at sea. He graphically termed it "the brothelization of the Navy." His outrage was not only leveled against profiteering "fleshmongers," but more especially against the lord commissioners of the Admiralty. He accused them of looking at such self-gratification as inevitable in order to prevent desertion. Smith's literary exposé in 1828, entitled *Portsmouth*, achieved wide publicity. By mid-century, when this type of "debauchery on demand" had finally been overcome, victory was largely credited to Smith's unflagging perseverance.

As to the situation for merchant mariners, it was only after coming to Sailortown himself that Smith was struck by the plight of "poor sea-har-lots." He eventually realized it was not enough to counsel these women in their hovels and preach to them in the streets. If such "Maritime Magdalenes" were to be rescued from the real criminals—the "Crimping Brothel-Owners"—more drastic measures were called for.

In the fall of 1829, seven prostitutes had responded to Smith's invitation to come to a service at the Mariners' Church. As they left the sanctuary, the girls cried and told him that they had no place to go but back to "walk the streets, and roll in infamy." In response, Smith helped establish a "Maritime Penitent Young Woman's Refuge" in Wellclose Square the following year, as a branch of the BFSSFS. Like the Sailors' Orphan House Establishment, it was at first partially operated by women in Smith's immediate family. It survived the upheaval in 1832 and resumed as an independent institution in Hackney Road. Meanwhile, Smith himself continued to campaign in print against this form of "Female Slave Trade," as he called it.

Meanwhile, Smith had been deeply impressed by a letter sent him in May 1829 by the leader of the American Seamen's Friend Society, Reverend Joshua Leavitt. Here, the writer expanded on "the most absorbing topic of enquiry agitating the United States at this time"—the question of "Temperance." Leavitt underscored that many American ships were "now navigating without grog." At the same time, he sent Smith a number of pamphlets and challenged him to start a comparable "reformation" on British ships.

Smith responded with enthusiasm, publishing a ninety-four-page pamphlet in the fall of 1829. Entitled *Intemperance,* it consisted largely of materials sent by Leavitt. The publication aroused such interest that it led to the launching of a general temperance movement in London and to the formation of "Temperance Societies" throughout the kingdom. A maritime version was founded at the Mariners' Church in June 1832. With Smith's eldest son, Theophilus, as an enthusiastic secretary, the society survived the summer storms that year, and was even expanded to include the military.

Once again encouraged by the American example, Smith and his associates took a further step in 1835, initiating a "Marine Temperance Movement" for the total abstinence from all intoxicating drinks. Three years later, this led to a "Sailors and Soldiers' Evangelical Temperance Society." In his magazine, Smith endorsed the belief that the word "teetotal" itself originated with an attendee at a meeting of the Preston Temperance Society in the early 1830s. As this "plain good man" explained—obviously excited to the point of stammering—nothing would do, but "tee-tee-total" abstinence. After which, all agreed that "teetotal" it must be.

Over the years, Smith developed a particularly warm relationship with Father Theobald Mathew (1790–1856), a Catholic priest born in Tipperary, who became widely known as Ireland's "Apostle of Temperance." Smith remained an active supporter of total abstinence for the rest of his life. He wrote about the intriguing "reciprocity" by which the Bethel Movement was brought from Britain to America, whereas the Marine Temperance Movement came from America to Britain.

The modern-day Alcoholics Anonymous Movement does not agree with Smith on the need for total abstinence for everyone. However, this latter movement has, since its foundation in 1935, consistently advocated for total abstinence from alcoholic beverages for all who are actually addicted to alcohol.

In spite of the impressive scope of all these activities, potential problems also appeared on the horizon. As the 1830s progressed, it became apparent that Smith's society, the British and Foreign Sailors' and Soldiers' Bethel Flag Union, was in serious financial straits. He changed the title back to the "British and Foreign Seamen and Soldiers' Friend Society." But he could not change the trend.

Despite wide support, debts from the 1832 disaster remained unpaid. Soon Smith stopped publishing annual accounts altogether, limiting himself to acknowledging only contributions. It did not improve matters when he charged the better patronized British and Foreign Sailors' Society with subverting his society and exaggerating the significance of their own.

For their part, the BFSS kept an official silence. From the close of 1834, however, there emerged another group of individuals who launched a campaign of undisguised resentment against Smith and his colleagues. First, there was Richard Carlile, the noted Fleet Street atheist. He lampooned Smith in his weekly *Scourge*, quoting liberally from the already rejected writings of Styles, Mead, and Sibree.

Then there was John Stephens, editor of the *Christian Advocate*, notorious for its religious sensationalism. Stephens put lurid extracts about Smith into book form under the title, *G. C. Smith Unmasked*. Here, the "Boatswain" was, to quote Smith himself, "hung, drawn and quartered… and the ashes scattered to the four winds."

It was the third assailant, a former "discarded agent" called John Harding, who proved to be the most persistent. Following his dismissal in 1835, Harding scattered leaflets filled with "wild claims" from *G. C. Smith Unmasked*. In March 1836, Harding managed to have Smith arrested for an alleged debt, while Smith was on a promotional tour in Buckinghamshire. As a result, Smith not only had to send back the group of singing seamen's orphans who would frequently accompany him on his trips, but he was himself incarcerated in the county prison at Aylesbury.

Despite all this, Smith was able to preach to his fellow prisoners every night. Later, he managed to obtain a transfer to the Fleet Street Prison in London, so as to be nearer his home and headquarters. At the latter prison he had to remain for three months before he was released. It was small consolation that the arbitrary Law of Imprisonment for Debt, which was then in force, would quite commonly commit also clergymen, officers, and "gentlemen of standing" to indefinite periods of mental and physical torture in debtors' jails. Nor did it change matters that, shortly afterwards, Harding was himself imprisoned, too.

No. 3086.   **JUNE, 1842.**   **VOL. 30**

Please to lend your Magazine after you have read it ; and aid the Cause by promoting its Circulation, and collecting ONE SHILLING for the General Cause, or for the Orphans, or for the Naval and Military Temperance Society, or Open Air Preaching Missions.

THE

Mariners' Church

GOSPEL TEMPERANCE

SOLDIERS' AND SAILORS'

MAGAZINE.

Published for the Temperance British and Foreign Seamen Soldiers', and Steamers' Friend Society and Bethel Flag Union, to promote Religious Instruction, and Temperance Moral Reformation.

THE LONDON MARINERS' CHURCH, WELLCLOSE SQUARE,
For Sailors, Soldiers, Fishermen, Watermen, and their Families.

Published at the Naval and Military Office, Bethel House, 17, Wellclose Square and by W. Brittain 11, Paternoster Row, and may be had of all Booksellers.

*** We beg to repeat that any Bookseller, in any Town, can order this Magazine, Monthly, in London, and throughout the United Kingdom.

PRICE 6d.

Smith's maritime mission magazine as published during his turbulent terms in debtors' prisons, 1836–45.

As for Smith, his jail time in 1836 was only the first in what became a series of four prison terms, all connected with clamoring creditors. Behind the bars of Queen's Bench Debtors' Prison, he would spend a further five months in 1840, seven months in 1843–44, and five months in 1845. All of this opened a new and challenging chapter of Smith's life. Although his writings contain many instances of arrest for open-air preaching, none of these had led to any long-term incarceration such as now.

A debtors' jail in the 1830–40s was still full of the stench and despair familiar from the writings of Charles Dickens. Nevertheless, it would take more than this to crush the spirit of a seasoned veteran from a Nelson man-of-war. While in jail, Smith persevered against all odds as editor of his *New Sailor's Magazine*. Also, with the help of family and friends, he managed to continue directing his society's general operations, which were still based in Wellclose Square.

Meanwhile, spurred by the degradation and spiritual neglect he saw around him, Smith even managed to launch a "Prison Howard Bethel Mission Society." Named after John Howard, the eighteenth century pioneer of prison reform, Smith's initiative was significant in a day when ministers generally "held aloof" from prison visitation altogether. Smith was encouraged by the cooperation of a fellow prisoner who happened to be "a clergyman of the Established Church." Still, his new society never did reach its declared goal—seeing the Bethel Flag unfurled over not only transport ships and prison hulks, but eventually prisons in general.

Smith's hardest blow came when he already had three prison terms behind him. He had stoutly refused to "give up the ship," as he called his church in Wellclose Square, until one fateful February morning in 1845. On the thirteenth day of that month, two lawyers who had been charged with enforcing the terms under which the church was rented suddenly descended on their luckless debtor. Armed with an order of eviction, they forced an entry into the church and had the minister arrested for non-payment of their expenses.

For Smith it did not make matters easier to learn that a new con-tract of rent had meanwhile been negotiated with his one-time "rival," the British and Foreign Sailors' Society. When Smith emerged from his final five months in the Queen's Bench Prison, all he had left was his magazine. That other indispensable asset, his church building, was—after twenty years of continuous service—now lost to him forever.

While in prison, it had been a great source of comfort for the "Boatswain Preacher" to have the support of not only fellow seafarers but also friends in his home port of Penzance. In addition, Smith recognized in his magazine what a deep impression it made on him when he received help during his imprisonment from Dr. Francis Cox, as well as other metropolitan ministers connected with the British and Foreign Sailors' Society.

After his release, Smith struggled on for three years, still ministering in London as best he could, despite "an ocean of troubles." Since his own home in Wellclose Square had by now become unlivable, he stayed in temporary lodgings here and there. Meanwhile, he carried on with his preaching and pastoral work—on the waterfront, in barracks, and on the streets. He even managed to work out of a makeshift maritime chapel where a few coworkers were trying to renew a Bethel outreach along Ratcliffe Highway.

The leader of that ministry, Reverend Gary Teil Hill, had been a close colleague of Smith during the critical years before his eviction. Following Smith's release in 1845, Hill asked for his help to fill the void left by Smith's former organization. January next year saw the founding of the "Seamen's Christian Friend Society" (SCFS), committed to promoting "Missions to Ships and in the Port of London, and on the Sea Coasts, to Barracks, Prisons and the Poor in general."

Smith frequently preached at this Society's first headquarters and "Seamen's Chapel." This was situated in a former sugar warehouse opposite the London Dock Gate on Ratcliffe Highway. Like the BFSS, the SCFS adopted a modified version of the Bethel Flag as its emblem. Based on its early cooperation with Smith, the SCFS has since been able to claim a personal, if not formal, link with the pioneer period of the Bethel Movement.

Meanwhile, Smith's lifestyle had become so fragmented that he realized a change was again called for. By the spring of 1848, his health had also clearly deteriorated. He therefore gladly accepted an opportunity to return to the milder climate and relative peace of Penzance—in order to resume his former pastorate at Jordan Chapel.

CHAPTER 13
BACK TO PENZANCE
(1848-1862)

For the final fifteen years of his life, Smith stayed in Penzance, the picturesque seaport in the southwest corner of Cornwall where he had once been ordained. However, despite his hopes for a more peaceful place than London, frustration would continue to hamper him throughout his declining years.

When Smith took up his appointment at Jordan Chapel in March 1848, it was in response to a unanimous call to be that congregation's resident pastor. Nevertheless, shortly after the sixty-six year old minister arrived, he launched forth, in characteristic style, with a whole series of additional initiatives: a Penzance Open Air Preaching Mission, a Penzance Town Mission, a Naval and Military Temperance Orphan Society, Sabbath Temperance Schools, and Sea Boys and Mariners' Girls Day Schools. In addition, he announced to his dazed flock that he would be gone six weeks every summer, touring south-coast port cities and returning via Bristol. As if that were not enough, he would be preaching from time to time elsewhere in Cornwall, as well as on the Islands of Scilly.

Apart from all such "external" activities, the church to which Smith returned was no longer the same as the Jordan Chapel he had left in 1826. During his absence, the chapel's leadership had been at odds with the regional Baptist Association. In 1834, a major part of the congregation had broken off in order to reestablish itself in Clarence Street—where it has continued ever since. As for the remaining portion of the chapel's congregation, the spirit of consensus among them on Smith's arrival in 1848 was soon shattered. Besides all who reacted to their pastor "dealing at great lengths with matters that were considered irrelevant," some saw his preaching as "insufficiently Calvinistic." Others were unhappy that he was not only so often away, but frequently preaching in the open air.

For five years Smith stayed his course. Though he went on spending several weeks each year on "Summer Missions" to London and along the sea coast, he also continued to minister as best he could to his flock at Jordan Chapel. As to Smith's domestic life, the 1851 Penzance Census states that his parsonage at 36 Parade Street included a housekeeper, her daughter, and ten orphan children—seven boys and three girls, between four and ten years old. For years, Smith had cared for up to twelve orphan children of sailors and soldiers, who supported his ministry with singing and in other ways. Not surprisingly, some of his adversaries tried to launch an abuse case against him. However, this was dismissed for lack of any evidence of wrongdoing.

In 1853, with Smith now into his seventies, he resigned from his congregation. This was due not only to his lengthy periods of absence, but also to his declining health and especially his financial stress. He then made the lower part of his private home, Jordan House, into a "Jordan Bethel Mariners' Church Temperance Hall." Also, as long as he carried on his annual stays in London, he rented Number 14 Wellclose Square as a home and headquarters there.

Research at the Morrab Library of Penzance has revealed that the Jordan Chapel was situated at the northeastern corner of the Morrab Gardens. Its precise location was at the front of St. Mary's Terrace, along South Parade at the rear—not actually on, but next to Chapel Street. In 1875, the chapel was finally closed. After being sold to the Public Rooms Company, the building was renovated as "a hall for entertainments." It then continued as "Regal Cinema" until this was demolished in the 1960s. Shortly afterward, the present Penlowarth Building was erected. This building belongs to the Inland Revenue and currently houses the local offices of the Department of Health and Social Services.

Available sources give only a fragmented picture of how Smith's family fitted into his turbulent life. In June 1808, Smith married Theodosia Skipwith, the daughter of John Skipwith, a well-known Yorkshire

Baptist. In his *Collectanea Cornubensia* (1890), George Clement Boase lists altogether six sons and four daughters born to the couple while in Penzance. There is no indication of how many survived to adulthood. However, in 1819, Smith wrote a remorseful, fifty-verse poem about the death of Cornelius, one of his three-year-old twin sons. The year before, the little boy had been "seized with the Croup" and died in his mother's arms while his father was away preaching somewhere near Land's End.

The familiar figure of "Bosun Smith," jovially depicted in silhouette in later years.
(Courtesy of Seamen's Christian Friend Society)

Inevitably, the move from a relatively peaceful Penzance to the squalid turmoil of London's Sailortown in 1826 was extremely stressful for Smith's family. He wrote that the constant human traffic through the cramped space of his rented home in Wellclose Square made it "more like a thoroughfare" than a human residence. During Smith's frequent travels, his family was "compelled to borrow even for the necessities of life." As they grew up, Smith's daughters would nonetheless attempt to help him, especially with practical and secretarial needs. This work was usually connected with their father's many sea-related societies for orphans, prostitutes, and their dependents.

Despite consistent solidarity on the part of Smith's daughters, this lifestyle must have been harrowing, not least for his wife, Theodosia. Despite the many children she cared for, she tried to maintain some vestige of domestic stability with her unpredictable life mate. Somehow she endured the many family and financial crises to which she was subjected over the years, including Smith's first two terms in prison. However, his third imprisonment became the last straw. In 1843, she left him.

Looking back in the November 1861 edition of his magazine, Smith writes about his relationship with his wife with uncharacteristic candor: "The unhappy difference between me and my wife commenced in 1840 [the second imprisonment], when an enemy had cruelly incarcerated me in prison on a false debt, because I was deprived of my salary. The entire separation of me and my wife from each other was in 1843 [the third imprisonment], when I was again most cruelly incarcerated by a bitter adversary." Smith goes on to share—in general terms—how an initiative from his side finally resulted in mutual forgiveness. He records the event under the title: "Domestic Forgiveness, Reconciliation, Peace, and Family Goodwill."

There also developed a more conciliatory tone in Smith's attitude to the British and Foreign Sailors' Society. After his second imprisonment, he even proposed "a union" of the two rival societies, his own and the BFSS. The plan was for the BFSS to "promote" the enterprise from their traditional headquarters at St. Mary Axe, while Smith would superintend "the working part" from Wellclose Square.

There is no record of any official response from the BFSS. As already noted, however, Smith did express warm appreciation in his magazine for the support he received during his incarceration from Dr. Francis Cox and other ministers connected with the BFSS. Also, Smith received a conciliatory letter in 1844 from Robert Humphrey Marten of the original Port of London Society.

Smith's change of attitude toward the BFSS was in part due to their opening of the London-based "Sailors' Institute" in July 1856. Situated on Mercers' Street, near Radcliffe Highway, it was soon known as the "Sailors' Palace." The multifaceted services of the Institute eventually became a model for similar institutions worldwide. With its Bethel Flag flying aloft, the building was, in fact, a fulfillment of George Charles Smith's own concept of a "Marine Guardian Establishment" launched a whole quarter century earlier. Here, for the first time, seafarers were now offered a spacious public hall, a reading room, library, refreshment room with "temperance" bar, a savings bank, and classrooms for day and navigation schools, all under one and the same roof.

While Smith openly commended the BFSS for this unique achievement, it was difficult for him to reconcile himself with the "abandonment" of the old Mariners' Church. Now that the BFSS had left for Mercer Street, this might well mean the surrender of Wellclose Square "to Satan"—the very scene of the enemy's "original garrison for soul-ruin, with all his immense armies of crimps and thieves and drunkards, and prostitutes, for the plunder and ruin of sailors and sea boys."

For Smith it made matters worse that it was the "Puseyite priests" from the Anglo-Catholic party of the established Church of England who had now taken over the Mariners' Church building. Despite his usual ecumenical spirit, Smith was quite unbending in his critique of these "Tractarians," as they were called, with all their "splendid dress and useless forms and ceremonies."

Smith continued his appeals for both divine and human intervention to help him resume his ministry from the Mariners' Church. In 1860, when he was close to eighty years of age, the indefatigable "Boatswain" was, according to his magazine, still hoping and planning to minister there again—fifteen years after his eviction. Shortly before, he had even visited the Danish and Swedish embassies in Belgrave Square—in a fruitless attempt to enlist their assistance on behalf of what was once a Dano-Norwegian church.

The London "Sailors' Institute," Mercer Street, Shadwell, popularly known as the "Sailors' Palace," opened in 1856 by the British and Foreign Sailors' Society, based on Smith's 1829 concept of a comprehensive "Maritime Guardian Establishment."

During his later years, Smith also had an overwhelming urge for what he called "usefulness overseas." In the New Year's issue of his 1855 magazine, he underscores how "the present extraordinary demand for Sailors and Soldiers, the dangers and deaths prevailing among them, and the unprecedented excitement in the British Empire for their families, demonstrate the necessity of Christian cooperation to do them good by all possible exertions." It was the controversial Crimean War of 1854–56 that was now absorbing the British nation.

The one-time volunteer chaplain from Wellington's Peninsular War in 1814 was not about to let his age prevent him from offering similar service in his country's new hour of need. In early 1855, Smith was prepared to cast off for Constantinople. To his disappointment, however, his offer was turned down. The official reason appears to have been lack of funds.

The outcome was no more successful in regard to his "Scandinavian Mission" in 1858–59. As Smith reminded his readership, he had once fought against the Danes, while serving under Admiral Nelson at the Battle of Copenhagen in 1801. He had at that time benefited from the willingness of the nearby Swedish fleets to withhold, when they could have descended on the battered British fleet after the battle. Now he hoped to return in the service of the Prince of Peace and bless these two nations by preaching along the coastlands of Denmark and Sweden. No doubt Smith also had in mind to press home his previous petition to the kings and governments of these nations for the restoration of the one-time Dano-Norwegian Church in London. Once again, however, the project foundered for lack of funds.

In contrast to these negative responses, Smith's third foreign project, his "American Sailors' Mission," became a resounding success. Many years earlier he had expressed his hope that the Lord would somehow let him "pay a three months visit to the United States, on a sailors, and soldiers and temperance, and open air orphans mission, to run down the coast from New York to New Orleans." He wrote this in 1844, during a respite between his third and fourth prison terms.

It would not be before the summer of 1861 that the old sailor would finally reach the New World. By all accounts, his visit turned into a triumphal tour. It was his British-born colleague in the US, Reverend Charles J. Jones, who coordinated Smith's engagements. Jones was the Presbyterian chaplain director of the New York Mariners' Church. He was also a former seafarer. While crossing the Atlantic by steamer from Liverpool, Smith made use of this as a golden opportunity to preach and counsel among fellow passengers and crew members.

In the course of his six-week stay, he was feted as the honored guest of seafarers' mission societies in six major port cities along the East Coast— New York, Philadelphia, Boston, Salem, Portland, and New Haven. More ready to accept his many eccentricities than his own countrymen had been, the Americans hailed him everywhere as the "Originator and Founder of the whole scheme of Bethel Union operations among Sailors."

In the *New York Sailor's Magazine* of September 1861, the editor included a report about how this "noble specimen of an old English sailor made his appearance in the Fulton Street prayer meeting," a place where Smith could still sense the afterglow of the great 1857 American revival. Here, as a former sailor under Admiral Nelson, he expressed his gratitude for the privilege of devoting over fifty years of his life to serve seafarers under "the Great Commander of our salvation."

It seemed nevertheless strange, Smith added, that when he finally arrived in America, he should find the nation at the outbreak of a devastating Civil War. All he could say was: "Let us go forth to battle, for some must go—and some must go never to return—but oh! Give me this place of prayer if I have any part to play in this matter."

In a subsequent account of Smith's visit to New York, Chaplain Jones describes how his guest commented somewhat wryly on how his voyage had become "the longest passage from Europe to America on record." Smith continued: "I sailed for America in 1796, in the brig Betsey, and have only reached it now in 1861. Sixty-five years is a long passage...." All of which was, of course, due to his brutal impressment by the British warship *Scipio* shortly before the *Betsey's* arrival in America.

Now that he had finally reached the New World, his many friends were determined to make the most of it. At each of the seaports he visited, he gladly responded to the Americans' unending appetite for the "Boatswain's" salty rhetoric about his life's work. In New York, Smith presented a Bethel Flag to the Episcopalians' Seamen's Church Institute, to be flown from the spire of their floating chapel. On the eve of his return to England, Smith's tour was crowned with the presentation of a silver commemorative medal. Presented by his host, Chaplain Jones, the medal bore the following inscription:

> This testimonial of our esteem and appreciation of his untiring and
> self-denying efforts for the salvation of the sailor, continued for
> nearly sixty years, is presented by friends in the Port of New York to

the Rev. George C. Smith, of Penzance, England, to commemorate his visit to the United States in the 80th year of his age, July 1861.

The other side of the medal is inscribed with the Greek text of Philippians 3:14—"I press on toward the goal." There is also a picture of a sailing ship surrounded with the hymn-lines, "Then in full sail my port I'll find, and leave the world and sin behind." (The medal has in recent years been in the custody of the Seamen's Christian Friend Society.)

After his return to England in the late summer of 1861, there were indications that Smith might be rediscovered by the religious community in his native land. No sooner had he landed in Liverpool, than the local Seamen's Friend Society—started by Smith himself forty years earlier—asked him to preach at three locations the same day, to give an account of the rise and progress of the work on both sides of the Atlantic.

As the winter continued into 1862. however, Smith found himself fighting a losing battle. It was becoming increasingly difficult for him to balance his boundless appetite for writing, traveling, and preaching with constantly mounting health and financial hardships.

Soon letters began appearing in the press. In the *British Standard*, for example, one writer wrote: "It is sad to reflect that after such toils and services to his fellow countrymen he should be found in circumstances of grinding poverty. In a day so fruitful of testimonials to men who one considered to have been great public benefactors it is strange that such a man as Mr. Smith should have been entirely overlooked." Another wrote in *The Revival:* "It is not enough to give such servants a pauper's relief; but help them to finish their work. No relief can give comfort to the soul of a 'Boatswain Smith' like success in labour."

Finally, a public subscription was launched for the relief of this "octogenarian veteran in the army of Emmanuel." At the same time, a petition for a pension, with 494 signatories, was delivered on his behalf to Lord Palmerston, the prime minister. Poignantly, both endeavors were launched too late for the old "Boatswain" to be able to benefit by either of them.

Smith's American Commemorative Medal, New York 1861.
(Custody of Seamen's Christian Friend Society)

CHAPTER 14
"LAST WATCH UPON DECK"
(1862–1863)

"I press on toward the goal!" It was meaningful that Smith's medal from New York should show this personal motto from the Apostle Paul. Nothing could have applied more aptly to the "Boatswain," as he lived through the final months that remained to him. Years ago, Smith had written that he was among those who had an inbuilt "natural steam engine"—every day propelling him forward. Once, he said, he had been "the same in the devil's service," only now he was in the Lord's.

As late as in 1860, Smith gave notice in his magazine that he was still "prepared and ready to return to Wellclose Square and East London, and take possession of the Mariners' Church, upon unsectarian, nonpolitical principles," that he might devote the remainder of his days "not as a man-of-war's man, but as a servant of the Prince of Peace, as a Sailors' and Soldiers' and Drunkards' and Magdalenes' Missionary."

At the same time, Smith's magazine continued to carry copious narratives of his "Sick Sailors' and Soldiers' Family Visitings" in the Penzance area. He also told of his latest open-air preaching, ship visiting and other local activities, not least in the cause of teetotalism.

The very fact that Smith's magazine was still appearing was in itself quite remarkable. After having launched *The Sailor's Magazine* in 1820 and then having to leave it to others in 1827, Smith had followed up with *The New Sailor's Magazine* the same year. The latter went through many titles over time, finally becoming *The Mariners' Church Gospel Temperance Sailors' and Soldiers' Magazine* in the year 1860. When Smith had to abandon his Mariners' Church in 1845, he determined that nothing would ever force him to hand over his last ministerial asset—his magazine. He resolved that his magazine would not expire before he did. That was a resolution he managed to keep.

The literary quality of Smith's magazine deteriorated, however, in later years. With frequent repetitions and so-called retrospects, it was also undeniably subjective. Still, when used critically, his magazine has remained highly relevant. Often it has been the only primary resource available. For his own part, Smith had great hopes for the magazine's historical potential. In 1858, as he completed his thirty-eighth volume, he wrote: "I consider them of the very utmost importance for future generations, as, long after I am dead, many will select [from them] the most remarkable events."

Smith had long since published his intent to follow the example of his childhood pastor, Rowland Hill, and one day "die in harness." That wish would be fulfilled. In his last *Sailors' and Soldiers' Magazine*, dated New Year 1863, he writes: "In closing the year 1862, I am in a strait, having a desire to depart and be with Christ. Nevertheless," he declares, paraphrasing Paul in Philippians 1:23–24, "to abide is more needful for many sailors and soldiers and sea-coast visiting." To this statement, he adds the following verse:

My last watch upon deck in this world now I keep
Very shortly expecting to lie down and sleep;
To awake up in glory, and with Christ to arise,
Free grace, endless glory, and all heaven my prize.

That was, indeed, his final message. On Saturday morning, January 10, 1863, George Charles Smith ended his "last watch upon deck," peacefully slipping away in his sleep. He had recently "suffered from the dropsy," it was reported. At first, the doctor had "some hopes" of him pulling through. But that was not to be.

Smith was, according to a Penzance colleague, "to the last full of active zeal for Christ and the salvation of souls." When his physical condition made him "no longer able to come down stairs, and preach to those who used to assemble at his house, he had them up to his bedroom, and desired them to read the Word of Life to him. On New Year's Eve he was brought downstairs and, after holding a watch-night service, he was carried up, with words of praise upon his lips for being spared to see the commencement of another year."

As might be expected, among those who had taken offense at the belligerent and fervent "Boatswain" over the years, there were some who gave public expression to their relief at his final passing. By contrast, only five days later, no less than *The Times* of London had this to say:

> DEATH OF BOATSWAIN SMITH. The Rev. G. C. Smith died at Penzance on Saturday morning, in his sleep, 81 years old. He was a prince of good men, warm-hearted, and a hard worker, and affected an immense amount of good in his day. There were no missions to seamen before he took the matter up, and founded seamen's chapels, sailors' homes, city missions.

The local historian, George Clement Boase, would later write: "One of the best answers to those who made reflections on 'Boatswain Smith's' management of money-matters is the fact that he died worth nothing whatever; and it was necessary for a few of his acquaintances to provide his remains with a coffin and a grave." In 1825, Smith had agreed with the Danish-Norwegian elders of the building that became the Mariners' Church that he would, in due course, be buried under the church's pulpit. As it happened, Smith was buried in Penzance Cemetery, St. Clare Street, on January 16, 1863.

There were good reasons for Penzance to be the resting place for the earthly remains of George Charles Smith. Not least was the fact that he lived in Penzance longer than in any other place. London was where Smith was both born and raised, and he would later live there for twelve years. Nonetheless, Penzance was Smith's hometown for thirty-four years, from 1807 to 1826 and from 1848 to 1863. Moreover, "The Rev. G. C. Smith, of Penzance" is how he was widely known on the title page of so many of his publications. Finally, it was clear that Smith himself, during his later years, accepted the port of Penzance as his point of departure for his "harbour forever."

According to one estimate, Smith's funeral was attended by some two-thousand mourners—an indication of his wide significance and the level of public affection, in spite of the many conflicts along the way. The funeral procession was preceded by five flags, headed by Alderman W. D. Mathews, the city's former mayor. It included detachments of both the Coastguard and Naval Reserve. Reportedly, "several Christian ministers" took part. Among these, an Independent church colleague delivered "a very appropriate address," while a Wesleyan minister offered a petition that the Lord might now, after George Charles Smith, raise up someone "to take his place in the rank, and like him fight valiantly for the cause of God and truth."

In March 1863, *The Gentlemen's Magazine* could report: "Since Mr. Smith's death, several meetings have been held in the West of England for the purpose of erecting a testimonial to his memory." The gravesite in Penzance Cemetery was, in fact, eventually marked by a headstone, listing the main facts and achievements of Smith's remarkable life.

The inscription on Smith's headstone refers to how he commenced his "ministrations to seamen" in Penzance, in response to a call from the Revenue Cruiser *Dolphin* in 1809. The inscription concludes: "His powers of mind and body were conservated to the spiritual and temporal welfare of British and Foreign Seamen. In this great work he led the way and originated nearly all the efforts put forth. . . . His life was that of an earnest self-denying servant of God and his death shewed the calm triumph of his faith."

Meanwhile, Smith's fellow worker, Reverend George Hill, who in 1846 went on to found the Seamen's Christian Friend Society, has recorded the following recollection from the "Boatswain's" heyday in London's Sailortown:

> I can picture him now as he walked down the Ratcliff Highway. He was a man of tremendous physique; tall, broad, deep-chested, with great biceps. He looked what he was, a strong man. He had the most powerful voice I ever heard and when he spoke in the old chapel he made the floorboards vibrate under our feet. He used to walk the roughest quarters in all London's maze of docks and was never harmed.

"Last Watch Upon Deck"

In July 1967, this author had the privilege of interviewing Violet Maud Rosier, a great-granddaughter of George Charles Smith, at her home in 34 Kensington Park Gardens, London. Her mother was one of "the three Smith sisters," daughters of Smith's eldest son, Theophilus. During our visit, she shared recollections of her great-grandfather's "thundering voice" and also his "powerful frame." She remembered when he came to visit his family in London: "His body was so broad that the usual half of the front door was too narrow, so they had to open up both halves for him."

Despite his exceptional physical attributes, Smith survived—as already recorded—three major illnesses during his adult life. First, in 1802, came his "riotous living," after his ship had anchored in Yarmouth Roads; this landed him in critical condition in the local Naval Hospital. Then, after recovering—to the surprise of his doctors—he shortly afterwards indulged in a new round of excessive drinking with his former shipmates. Finally, in 1803, when the fragile Peace of Amiens began to crumble, Smith went on to tell how he was again laid low, this time by "a virulent fever." He was then staying at the public house "Jack of Newbury" in Reading, where he had been seeking respite from a recently revived impressment campaign.

In addition to these self-inflicted cases, Smith recorded having been "confined to bed by sickness" in 1811, during his early pastorate in Penzance. He also frequently referred to health-related incidents in reports from his constant travels. For example, in 1832 he came home with an "inflammatory fever" that reduced him for a while to "a wreck dashing against the rocks upon a lee shore." As late as in 1858, preaching in the open air in Blackheath, London, he was "severely injured" when an intoxicated man ran a cart over both his legs.

It goes without saying that the stress-filled controversies in which Smith became involved during so much of his life must have taken a severe toll on his psychological—and probably also physical—state of health. Finally, illustrations in later years depict the "Boatswain" with a body weight that must have been a considerable additional challenge.

Taking all such factors into consideration, it seems strange that Smith was not laid low far earlier in his turbulent life. Eighty years of age was certainly well above normal male longevity in the mid-1800s. As one colleague pointed out, for any person to endeavor "that which the whole Christian world feared to attempt," such a task did indeed call for all the "powers of mind and body" that came to characterize the life of George Charles Smith, the "Boatswain Pastor of Penzance."

CHAPTER 15
THE LEGACY OF GEORGE CHARLES SMITH:
A SUMMARY

"Our history now belongs to posterity." So wrote George Charles Smith as he looked back at his life. In the years immediately following his death, the nature of his legacy was seen in very different ways. In America, Smith was compared with the role of the Reformation's fourteenth century forerunner, John Wycliffe; there, he was widely acclaimed as the "Morning Star of the Sailor's Reformation." In England, there were those who saw Smith rather as "an erratic comet." Although some of his compatriots gave him recognition, even if muted, others chose simply to ignore him. How, then, is the life of George Charles Smith to be fairly appraised in the light of later research?

As Smith himself saw it, his adversaries had for long been unloading onto him whole "shiploads of calumny on every shore." Many of the charges against him were clearly unfounded. Others were exaggerated. But dishonesty was never among them. Nonetheless, it would be wrong to insist there was no trace of truth in any of them. In at least two ways, he was himself responsible for the misfortunes that overtook him in his later years.

In the first place, the sporadic belligerence of this burly sailor pastor—notorious for his "oceanic" temperament—made him many enemies. As one Penzance author put it: "'Boatswain Smith' was one of those men who always seemed to be in hot water. From the earliest times he had enemies; and he continued to have enemies all his days."

Once convinced of the justice of his cause, the navy veteran would just hurl himself into the fray—without the least regard for who the "enemy" happened to be, or how impossible the odds. For example, as early as in 1821, Smith brushed off any who opposed his battle for the Bethel Flag by alluding to his service in the foretop of a man-of-war. Never would he have refused "to go aloft for fear of being washed off or having his head shot off." Again, as already noted, he rejected whatever "broadside" his adversaries might deliver by asking: Why should one who had "stood the fire of the hottest cannon now be afraid of squibs and crackers"?

Secondly, Smith's eccentricity was self-evident. An example is the degree "B.B.U." that he conferred upon himself while incarcerated at the Queen's Bench Prison in 1840. Standing for "Burning Bush Unconsumed" from Exodus 3, this reference to the Old Testament's indefatigable God of Sinai was Smith's way of ridiculing adversaries with more formal education than his. In his later publications, Smith would even expand the letters after his name to "R.N.B.B.U.," so as to include his service in the Royal Navy.

Of course, eccentricity might well go hand in hand with ingenuity. In Victorian England, however, Smith's behavior seemed to ignore contemporary criteria for "respectability." This was still a nation where a well-known hymn stanza voiced a virtually "theological" rationale for the place of birth and heredity in society: "The rich man in his castle, the poor man at his gate, God made them high and lowly and ordered their estate." Following the collapse of Smith's organization in 1832, he alienated himself even further from the patronage of fellow ministers with expressions such as "high mightinesses of dissent."

In addition to his belligerence and eccentricity, one might include Smith's chronic inability to keep regular accounts. He was the target of public complaints as early as during his subscription campaign on behalf of the destitute on the Scilly Islands. No satisfactory accounts were rendered and Smith was never able to provide adequate documentation.

The local historian, G. C. Boase, suggests a benign and plausible explanation: "When his pity was moved, [he] gave away money and was then so occupied with other business that he forgot to make an entry of the circumstances. At all events, he never made any money or saved any." As for Smith himself, he once wrote that he thanked God for the last year's many "sources of expenditure"—without one word about possible sources of income!

At times, Smith could candidly confess his shortcomings—at least in a generic sense. He once declared: "I have a thousand evils before God to mourn over." To which he added: "May the good Lord pardon all he has seen amiss." Still, whatever failings he may have had, nothing can alter the magnitude of innovative accomplishments for which this one person was instrumental.

Smith was not the originator of "seafarers' mission" as such. Beginning with the early church, there is evidence of many prior forms of Christian ministry among sailors through the centuries. Nonetheless, not before the second decade of the nineteenth century was there any sustained effort in an organizational sense. In relation to the latter movement, George Charles Smith has remained the pivotal pioneer personality.

Seeing Smith as "Founder of Seafarers' Mission" may be a subject for debate, all according to one's definition of seafarers' mission. As "Founder of the Seafarers' Mission Movement," Smith remains indisputable. Based on all available sources, nobody has come even close to him in terms of individual significance for the early evolution of mission among people of the sea.

In that role, Smith was not primarily a systematic theologian seeking to build a theoretical "Maritime Missiology." His purpose was practical—specifically centered around the global potential of the Bethel Flag, with its limitless implications for outreach. It was thanks to George Charles Smith that the lay-led Bethel Movement ultimately became the core of the nineteenth-century Seafarers' Mission Movement.

As in the case of all great innovations, the key to Smith's success seems to have been a case of the right person appearing at the right time. Here was a historic convergence of those two basic preconditions for any form of positive change—competence and context.

In regard to competence, George Charles Smith became "The Sailors' Preacher" of his age. His rhetorical gifts were widely recognized as extraordinary. He could pour out "threatenings in sounds like thunder," and yet entreat "reckless sinners" to be reconciled to God, "with tears coursing down his face, his whole frame quivering." Smith himself loved to use his gifts as preacher—whether among seafarers or elsewhere.

Smith's eldest son, Theophilus, has recorded how his father was harassed for his practice of open-air preaching throughout much of his life. This was an age when civic authorities had not yet recognized the human right to communicate religious or other convictions in public. It helped little that *The Times* of London had early on hailed Smith as "the prince of field preachers." It was only after he had been arrested again and again for this "crime"—and even formed a "British Open-air and Annual Fair Preaching Society"—that the police were finally "compelled to desist from their persecutions."

The following is an example of Smith's ingenuity when faced with arbitrary authority. During the public fair that was regularly held in Bristol, Smith would preach in the open space in front of St. James' Church. It would normally be filled with various shows and big crowds. On one occasion, a constable was charged by the town magistrate to prevent Smith from preaching. When he took his place at the appointed time and the constable ordered him not to preach, Smith politely asked, "Will you allow me to tell these people why I cannot preach?" To this the constable gave his ready assent.

"Boatswain Smith" then began: "My friends, I came here intending to preach to you from those solemn words, Flee from the wrath to come! I meant to have told whose wrath you must flee from. But my friend here says I must not. I meant to have told you why you should flee from this wrath to come—even to the Lord Jesus Christ, the Savior of poor lost sinners. But I cannot do what I would, for the constable says 'No!'" In this manner he managed to preach the entire sermon.

When he had finished, Smith turned to the constable and said, "Now, Mr. Constable, you will not, I am sure, object to my properly dismissing these people?" "Oh dear no; certainly not, Sir." "Then," said the "Boatswain," "let us sing Praise God from Whom all Blessings Flow!" When this had been well and truly sung by the crowd, he offered a brief prayer and, with a smile, received the thanks of the constable for being so good as to comply with his instructions without giving the slightest trouble.

Despite his general popularity wherever he preached, it was especially among fellow seafarers that Smith would make his mark. In this context, it would be difficult to overestimate the significance of his years of personal experience at sea. For the thousands of mariners who flocked to hear him, it was the ring of authenticity in his masterly use of nautical language that made them recognize him as one of their own—one who quite literally "knew the ropes."

They said as much when they asked him to preach for them, those storm-tossed sailors on a revenue cutter in Penzance in early 1809; their response became his call to devote his future ministry to seafarers' mission. They also said as much, those mariners on the Thames in 1817, who introduced Smith to the Bethel Movement; they flocked to hear him, and their cause became his for the rest of his life.

Besides becoming a preeminent preacher, George Charles Smith was also "The Sailors' Advocate" of his day. This was an age when this whole class of humanity was still ostracized by church and society as "a race apart," unfit for the benefits of humans at large. Here, too, Smith could contribute from his familiarity with the seafarer's distinctive subculture. This helped him to promote a methodology of ministry which, for the first time in history, seriously addressed his fellow seafarers' most pressing needs.

Even though Smith's vision of a "Marine Jerusalem" far outpaced his ability to deliver, he was in many respects a forerunner in the field of Maritime Sociology. Above all, he proved that seafarers, as well as their dependents ashore, were so socially and spiritually isolated that they could never be adequately reached by conventional shore-based models of ministry.

In following his vocation, Smith found his focus had to be single-minded. This could sometimes leave him single-handed—and therefore vulnerable. This did not mean he was narrow-minded. In spite of his boisterous temperament, Smith was no religious fanatic—although he might seem so. Nor was he a life-negating spiritualist. Smith's overriding concern was to make the Christian gospel universally available, while reminding his hearers about the eternal implications of a personal response.

Smith was also "holistic" in his concept of mission—integrating both social concerns and systemic change. Just as seafarers had "no soul-less bodies," he also insisted they had "no body-less souls." There was no point in preaching to penniless sailors or prostitutes while watching them perish for want of the barest necessities of life. Smith was relentless in his exposure and attack on the underlying cause of poverty—the notorious "Crimping System" and its chokehold on the whole maritime industry.

Nevertheless, for this "Sailors' Preacher and Advocate," competence alone could not possibly explain his unparalleled achievements. There was also the issue of context. It could well be argued that the overall context in which George Charles Smith found himself could hardly have been more favorable. This applied to both when and where he came on the scene.

As to the issue of time, when Smith launched forth in the early 1800s, it was immediately after the spiritual awakenings that washed over both Britain and America during the latter part of the preceding century. Of special relevance just then was the lay-based support group system of the revival campaign led by the Methodist leader, John Wesley. Smith insisted it was the Wesleyan Methodists that "God was pleased to honour to start this great work." By that he specifically included the origin of the Bethel Flag.

Yet, when all was said and done, a "Boatswain Smith" was still needed to make the Bethel Flag the emblem of a worldwide "Bethel Movement." Again, it was Smith who needed to be there to initiate a maritime version of the "voluntary society" model, which by then had become the structural vehicle for the spiritual awakenings in Britain and America. Beginning with the Port of London Society in 1818, Smith started, as we have seen, a whole series of new societies—even though his notorious lack of funds meant he would have to leave it to others to continue them.

As for the place where it all began, it was understandable that Britain became the primary site of the early Seafarers' Mission Movement.

After the Battle of Trafalgar in 1805, it was Britannia who literally "ruled the waves." With his recent service in the Napoleonic War Royal Navy, Smith was well positioned to speak to the critical role of seafarers in defense of his island nation's security. He could also address with passion the potential role of seafarers in his country's new concern for world mission. This had already been stimulated by the recent South Seas discoveries of Smith's fellow Yorkshire-man, Captain James Cook.

From the early 1820s, through contact by visitors, letters and his magazine, Smith was readily recognized by pioneers on the other side of the Atlantic as a personal mentor. It seems likely that both sociological and ecclesiological reasons contributed to this. Born in 1782, only months after the decisive victory of the American revolutionaries at Yorktown, Smith was in many respects a lifelong rebel. Ever ready to champion the cause of the underdog against whatever he perceived to be abuse of authority, whether in government, church, or society, Smith was continuously at odds with established norms.

As to religion, Smith would, as far as England was concerned, downplay his personal choice of Baptist—and therefore "Dissenter"—affiliation. In the multi-denominational United States, however, established religion had become a thing of the past. At all events, America's Baptists were currently increasing at such a rate that identifying with them was in no sense seen as a disadvantage.

It was not surprising that a dynamic and diversified New World was more ready to accept a colorful, unconventional character like Smith. With all his eccentricities, Smith somehow "fitted in" more easily among Americans than among his more tradition-conscious compatriots in England. Nonetheless, one may well wonder which direction Smith's life would have taken, if a fourteen-year-old greenhorn had not been prevented from reaching Boston on the *Betsey* back in 1796—in other words without first going through those seven years of tough naval "schooling."

Down the years, Smith's accomplishments gained greater recognition in the Old World, too. The words of an American colleague, originally spoken in the thick of controversy on the London scene in 1830, would eventually be vindicated on both sides of the Atlantic: "Posterity will not willingly allow either detraction or demerit to erase from the scroll of Christian worthies the name of the Rev. G. C. Smith of Penzance."

Beyond Smith's role as founder of the Maritime Mission Movement, the ultimate test of his standing has to be his relevance to the seafaring world of succeeding generations. In what ways do Smith's achievements have any significant bearing on the current and future scene? With the impact of globalization, automation, containerization, and a host of other factors, today's maritime situation is vastly different from the seafaring world of Smith's day. Still, there are some important parallels. These transcend both time and space and give remarkable relevance to strategies Smith developed in the early nineteenth century.

When Smith took up his formidable challenge, to bring the gospel of Christ to the life and world of seafarers, he knew only too well their problems of deprivation, both materially and spiritually. Materially, seafarers of his day—and still for decades to come—were treated like slaves, with an average life expectancy of no more than twelve years after going to sea. Some speculated seriously that a seafarer must belong to a separate species—bereft of a human soul. Smith accused the churches of treating so-called heathens overseas with greater concern than spiritually starved seafarers in their own port cities.

Today's seafaring world shows some strikingly similar traits. With international tonnage transferring to "flags-of-convenience," low-cost, largely Asian maritime labor has taken over much of the global workforce at sea. This has resulted in escalating exploitation and the violation of the most basic human rights of large numbers of seafarers. Due to such ship's crews usually being nonunionized, or at best only weakly represented, they are especially vulnerable. Also, since a large number of today's seafarers are adherents of non-Christian faiths, the background is a context of religious pluralism. For many, this is accompanied by a high level of spiritual searching.

As a result, the two overriding theological challenges in modern-day maritime mission are the same as confronted Smith in the early 1800s. On the one hand, there is a vital need for social justice for all and on the other, an equally clear need for sensitive evangelism—one marked by mutual respect and unconditional love.

Smith combined a program of innovative institutions and public advocacy, to meet a level of need even his adversaries could not deny. Through the 1820s and into the 1830s, Smith proposed one institution or initiative after the other—for the benefit of uneducated, unemployed, sick and aging sailors and their families, as well as for prostitutes and even the crimps who victimized them.

As the "Sailor's Advocate," Smith fearlessly addressed admirals, bishops, police, politicians, even Queen Victoria—anyone in a position of power. He admitted that at times he "did write much too strong." But whatever his critics might allege, no one was able to prove him guilty of either financial fraud or abuse of the powerless.

Smith's role was unique in the sense that he gave a global reach to the Bethel Movement. From his Rotherhithe days in 1817 and throughout his life, Smith maintained the vision of seafarers rallying around the Bethel Flag and taking the principle responsibility for mission among their own and around the world.

Yet, although seafarers always remained primary, Smith's concern was never narrowly exclusive. He wholeheartedly embraced everyone— soldiers, prisoners, "foreigners" (including China's millions), as well as any with an underprivileged position in society. He likewise included the addicted—not only alcohol abusers, but also tobacco users. (The latter seems almost ironic, given the belief that tobacco was first smoked in England when Sir Walter Raleigh celebrated his return from Virginia by puffing from his pipe on a pier in precisely Penzance!)

Although Smith had little patience for high church rituals, he was no dedicated denominationalist. He was, for example, constantly cajoling the Church of England to take a more active responsibility for its own Anglican-affiliated seafarers. As for relations with the Roman Catholics, anti-Catholic prejudice was—despite the Catholic Relief Act of 1829—still rampant in the United Kingdom of Smith's day. However, his long and close collaboration with Father Theobald Mathew, Ireland's

"Apostle of Temperance," gave ample proof of where Smith stood against religious discrimination.

The Penzance historian G. C. Boase, in his sketch on "Boatswain Smith," comments as follows: "Despite the many conflicts in his life, probably, according to modern ideas, he was generally in the right; possibly he was somewhat in advance of his age." For Smith, evangelism, diaconal care, and advocacy were all three inseparable dimensions— precisely as in current-day concepts of authentic maritime mission.

The renovated gravestone of George Charles Smith at Penzance Cemetery under a Bethel Flag unfurled in October 2004 by Dr. Stephen Friend, cofounder of the International Association for the Study of Maritime Mission.

Perhaps the most powerful affirmation of Smith's continuing relevancy—and therefore modernity—is the level of interest that his life and work has generated among recently formed non-Western maritime missions. As these have come onto the scene, all of them have discerned in George Charles Smith the profile of a prophet.

The Legacy of George Charles Smith

In England, Smith's status was publicly affirmed in October 2004 by a colorful commemoration of his life and work at his gravesite in Penzance. The ceremony recognized the 200th anniversary of Smith's call to the ministry in 1804. The event was attended by the mayor of Penzance, local ministers, and deputations from the Coastguard, the British Legion, and the Fishermen's Mission. It was given full-page exposure in the *Penzance Press* and wide coverage by the British Broadcasting Corporation.

The ceremony was sponsored by the modern-day version of Smith's earliest society, the Southampton-based (British and International) Sailors' Society, and led by Reverend David Potterton, its principal chaplain. The event was also facilitated by the International Association for the Study of Maritime Mission (IASMM). On behalf of the latter, this author pointed to how the current global era's "New Bethel Movement" has evolved as a remarkable revival of Smith's original Bethel Movement of the early 1800s.

The same year would see the present day New Bethel Movement formally affirmed in academic research. In recent years, Smith's prophetic role had already been recognized in the dissertations of Korean researchers like Jonah Choi, David Chul-Han Jun, and Byeong-Eun Lee. Then, in 2004, it was for the first time analyzed in a more comprehensive manner by Dean Paul Mooney of New Ross, Ireland, in a ThD dissertation published under the title, *Maritime Mission: History, Developments, A New Perspective.*

Paul Mooney's research was hailed in a review in the International Association for the Study of Maritime Mission as a "Watershed Event in Maritime Missiology." As Mooney put it, the changed context of current-day maritime industry calls for a radical shift in maritime ministry. This means moving from a shore-based, chaplain-centered model by empowering seafarers themselves to minister among their own on shipboard—in a renewed modern-day version of the original Bethel Movement.

All of which leaves shoreside seafarers' centers free to fill a cooperating role rather than a dominating one. Most importantly, it demonstrates in a dramatic way the continuing relevancy of Smith's core contribution to maritime mission: seeing seafarers not as objects but subjects of mission.

In other words, seafarers as key partners in a New Bethel Movement—with peer ministry at sea providing the main means of fulfilling Christ's Great Commission in the seafaring world.

Dr. Stephen Friend has, in his maritime mission research, pointed to the tendency for controversy evident among many pioneer mission personalities. An embattled Smith once said of himself in the heat of public conflict: "Rough men are required for rough work." True, Smith was a rough diamond—but nonetheless a diamond. He not only overcame incredible adversity as he sought to sensitize the church to her responsibility for the evangelization of the seafarer and the humanization of the maritime industry. He pressed on to become a "Sailors' Preacher" and a "Sailors' Advocate" such as the world has never seen—before or since.

It was indeed a "wind of change" that confronted a former Nelson sailor when hailed by those storm-tossed fellow mariners in the port of Penzance in 1809. Since then, if the glory of the Lord is one day to "cover the earth as the waters cover the sea," future generations will never be able to ignore the prophetic legacy of George Charles Smith.

ADDENDUM

JOHN NEWTON AND GEORGE CHARLES SMITH: LINKS BETWEEN A FORMER SLAVE SHIP CAPTAIN AND A FORMER NELSON SAILOR

No biography of George Charles Smith would do justice to one acclaimed as the "Prince of Field Preachers" without comparing him with the most beloved British preacher of his day, Reverend John Newton (1725–1807). This not least because of the prayers of Smith's mother, that her unruly son would one day become "like Newton, a great preacher of the gospel to perishing sinners."

Smith and his predecessor had much in common. They were both dramatic examples of what Tolkien calls "eucatastrophe"—when something spectacularly good happens to someone spectacularly bad. This would cause each of them to marvel, when looking back in later years. Otherwise, besides having devout mothers, both shared a seafaring background—including the harrowing experience of impressment into the Royal Navy.

Less widely known is the nature of the twofold religious renewal they both went through. After what some, including Jim Wallis, have called a "first conversion" from practical godlessness, there was, in both cases, a long lapse before this initial spiritual awakening was succeeded by a more profound "second conversion"—one characterized by a clear and consistent change in moral behavior.

This phenomenon is identified in Scripture as evidence of sincere repentance, expressed in a changed lifestyle (Matt 3:8, Acts 26:20). Here, Newton and Smith would both need mature mentors. They also both found themselves praying that the Lord would one day lead them into a vocation more compatible with their new direction of life.

THE TWO SIGNIFICANT WOMEN IN NEWTON'S LIFE

In 1764, John Newton wrote a series of fourteen letters to an influential friend, the Reverend Dr. Thomas Haweis. The letters were reproduced in book form under the title, *An Authentic Narrative of Some Remarkable Particulars in the Life of John Newton*. The book became immediately popular, and was later published under the title of the opening words of Psalm 130, *Out of the Depths: Autobiography of the Rev. John Newton*. Quotations below, from Newton's turbulent journey of life up to 1764, are from this latter autobiography.

Newton began his story by telling about the deep impact of two women in his life. In relation to his mother, Elizabeth Newton, he retained a warm and vivid memory of her as long as he lived. As he put it:

> I was her only child. Almost all her whole employment was the care of my education. When I was four years old I could read with propriety in any common book. She stored my memory with many valuable portions of Scripture, catechisms, hymns, and poems. My mother intended from the first to bring me up with a view to the ministry, if the Lord should so incline my heart. In my sixth year I began to learn Latin.

In 1732, those plans were shattered, when Newton's mother died of tuberculosis, just a few days before her son was seven years old.

Newton also described how a disinterested stepmother, a cruel boarding school, and—from the age of eleven—sea-time under the captaincy of a moralistic father, severely undermined his childhood faith. Besides his mother, the only other person who would make an indelible impression on him was Mary Catlett. It was ten years after his mother's death that he met her for the first time.

In 1742, a merchant friend of Newton's father in Liverpool suggested sending him to Jamaica to learn to be a slave master on a sugar plantation. Before leaving, Newton was invited to visit some good friends of his mother at Chatham in Kent—George and Elizabeth Catlett. As soon as he saw their almost fourteen-year-old daughter Mary, the seventeen-year-old John Newton found himself helplessly in love.

Addendum

In his memoirs Newton stated: "I felt an affection for her which never abated or lost its influence a single moment in my heart. I soon lost all sense of religion, and became deaf to the remonstrances of conscience. But none of the misery I experienced ever banished her a single hour from my waking thoughts for seven years following."

NEWTON'S DISCOVERY OF GRACE

During those seven years, Newton suffered a succession of trials, which as he later wrote, "made shipwreck of faith, hope and conscience." Forced by a press-gang onto a man-of-war, the HMS *Harwich*, he tried a short while later to escape. On being caught, he was flogged nearly to death and demoted from midshipman to common sailor. "Brought down to a level with the lowest, and exposed to the insults of all," he could later tell how he at this time seriously contemplated suicide. It was the memory of Mary that held him back: "My love was now the only restraint I had left. Though I neither feared God nor regarded men, I could not bear that she should think meanly of me when I was dead."

Eventually, Newton managed to obtain a transfer to a slave ship whose captain happened to know Newton's father. On reaching Sierra Leone in West Africa, Newton grasped an opportunity to take employment with a local slave trader on the Plantane Islands. During the slave trader's absence, however, Newton was left to the mercy of this man's jealous African mistress. Under her constant abuse, he again came close to death—this time from acute fever and hunger. Newton would later refer to himself during that period as "a servant of slaves in Africa."

Early in 1747, thanks to a captain his father had asked to help search for his son, Newton was able to embark on a trading ship ultimately bound for Britain. While this vessel, the *Greyhound*, was still taking on various kinds of cargo along the African coast, Newton admits he lapsed into "the most horrid impiety and profaneness." It went so far that the captain deplored he had taken "a Jonah on board."

Then, in March of the next year, Newton came across a copy of Thomas a Kempis' *Imitation of Christ*—the Catholic devotional, which had once affected John Wesley so deeply. In dismay, Newton found himself asking: "What if these things should be true?" With that, he hurriedly laid the book aside. "But now" he later found reason to add, "the Lord's time was come."

> I went to bed that night in my usual security and indifference, but was awakened by the force of a violent sea, which broke on us. Much of it came down below and filled the cabin where I lay with water. March 21 is a day I have never suffered to pass wholly unnoticed since the year 1748. On that day the Lord sent from on high and delivered me out of deep waters. I continued at the pump from three in the morning till near noon, and then I could do no more. Not being able to pump, I went to the helm, and steered the ship till midnight. I here had opportunity to think of my former religious professions, the warnings and deliverances, the licentious course of my life. I waited with fear and impatience to receive my inevitable doom.
>
> When I saw beyond all probability there was still hope of respite, and heard about six in the evening that the ship was freed from water, there arose a gleam of hope. I thought I saw the hand of God displayed in our favour and I began to pray. I could not draw near to a reconciled God and call Him Father. My prayer was like the cry of ravens, which yet the Lord does not disdain to hear. I now began to think of that Jesus whom I had so often derided. I recollected the particulars of His life and of His death—a death for sins not His own, but for those who in their distress should put their trust in Him.

Finally, with only "clothes and bedding to stop the leaks," with the ship's sails "mostly blown away," and with "the very last victuals boiling in the pot," Newton describes how the vessel managed to limp into shelter in Lough Swilly, in northwest Ireland.

Meanwhile, Newton realized: "The Lord had wrought a marvelous thing. I was no longer an infidel. I was freed from the habit of swearing which seemed to have been deeply rooted in me as a second nature. To all appearances, I was a new man. I could no more make a mock of sin, or jest with holy things. I consider this as the beginning of my return to God, or rather of His return to me. But," Newton underscored, "I cannot consider myself to have been a believer in the full sense of the word till a considerable time afterwards."

At last, in late May 1748, Newton arrived in Liverpool. He was too late to see his father, who had hoped to have his son accompany him to his new post as governor of York Fort in Hudson's Bay. Instead, a friend of his father secured Newton a position as first mate on a slave-trading vessel, the *Brownlow*, bound for West Africa.

It was during this time that Newton began to acknowledge the inadequacy of his spiritual life. "By the time I arrived at Guinea," he later admitted, "I seemed to have forgotten all the Lord's mercies. Profaneness excepted, I was almost as bad as before." He had not yet recognized he was "incapable of standing a single hour without fresh supplies of strength and grace from the fountain-head." Newton continued:

> While upon the coast, my business was to sail from place to place in the longboat to purchase slaves. The ship was at Sierra Leone, and I was then at the Plantanes, the scene of my former captivity. I was in easy circumstances, courted by those who formerly despised me.
>
> But the Lord again interposed to save me. He visited me with a violent fever, which once more brought me to myself. Weak and almost delirious, I arose from my bed and crept to a secluded part of the island; there I found a renewed liberty to pray. I made no more resolves, but cast myself before the Lord to do with me as He should please. I was enabled to hope and believe in a crucified Saviour, and not only my peace but my health was restored. I returned to the ship two days afterwards. From that time, His powerful grace has preserved me.

During eight further months on the coast, Newton felt he was granted grace through countless escapes from physical dangers, too. These included violence by resistant natives and repeated overturning in canoes—without knowing how to swim. Grateful for all he had witnessed of the Lord's "wonderful providence," Newton eventually returned to Liverpool. As soon as he was free to leave, he headed down to Kent. There, seven years after he first met Mary, they were finally joined in marriage on February 1, 1750.

GEORGE CHARLES SMITH OF PENZANCE

NEWTON'S BELATED REJECTION OF SLAVERY

It would take time before Newton's experience of grace led to a discovery of its implications in daily life—not least in regard to slavery. In his letters to Dr. Haweis, Newton shows it was taken for granted that he would, after his marriage, continue his seafaring career. At this point, he also assumed that this would still be in the slave trade. Looking back, Newton wrote:

> During the time I was engaged in the slave trade, I never had the least scruple as to its lawfulness. I was upon the whole satisfied with it as the appointment providence had marked out for me. It was, indeed, accounted a genteel employment. However, I considered myself as a sort of jailer and I was sometimes shocked with an employment that was perpetually connected with chains, bolts, and shackles. In this view I had often prayed that the Lord in His own time would be pleased to place me in a more humane calling, and where I might have more frequent fellowship with His people.

After leaving for sea again in November 1750, Newton sailed for the first time in command of his own slave ship, first the *Duke of Argyle*, subsequently the *African*. It was as captain of the latter, during the spring of 1754 at St. Kitt's (St. Christopher's) in the West Indies, that Newton happened to meet a Scottish captain by the name of Alexander Clunie. Here was a fellow captain who, by contrast, was not engaged in the slave trade. At the same time, this was a person who would have a profound spiritual effect on Newton, being the first close Christian friend he ever had.

It was Captain Clunie who helped Newton to discover the blessing of Christian fellowship. Newton wrote:

> For nearly a month, we spent every evening together on board each other's ship alternatively. I was all ear; he not only increased my understanding, but his teaching warmed my heart. He encouraged me to open my mouth in social prayer. He taught me the advantage of Christian conversation, to make my profession more public, and to venture to speak for God. I was delivered from a fear, which had long troubled me—the fear of relapsing into my former apostasy. Now I began to understand the security of the covenant of grace, through faith in an unchangeable Saviour.

Addendum

Clunie also supplied Newton with many Christian contacts. These included Dr. David Jennings, who had once been pastor of the Independent Meeting House in London's Sailortown suburb of Wapping. Newton's mother had been a member there and had also brought her son to baptism in the meeting house in July 1725. Newton would continue to correspond frequently with both Captain Clunie and Dr. Jennings.

Some modern writers have accused Newton of hypocrisy for personally participating in slave trading long after claiming to have become a Christian. However, for years there is no evidence that Newton had any problem with seeing slavery as quite compatible with Christian faith—like so many ill-informed Christians in his day.

Newton never identified the precise time at which his views on the slave trade changed—from permissiveness to abhorrence. There is no doubt he must have been deeply impacted by certain people whose views were very different from his own. Long before Newton knew of Captain Clunie's position, he was already well aware of his sweetheart Mary's deep disgust for the horrors of the slave trade. Doubtless the gathering momentum of the Slave Trade Abolition Movement must also have played a major role. Perhaps most of all, Newton's diligent study of Scripture had its transformative effect. He came to realize it made no sense to reduce fellow humans, for whom Christ had also died, to subhuman property fit only for profit and exploitation.

In his autobiography, Newton included the story of how his career as a slave ship captain came to an abrupt end—especially how it happened without the least moral consideration. The time was shortly after his arrival home in 1754:

> I was within two days of sailing, and to all appearances in good health as usual. In the afternoon as I was sitting with Mrs. Newton drinking tea, and talking over past events, I was taken by a seizure which deprived me of sense and motion. It lasted about an hour. When I recovered, a pain and dizziness in my head induced the physicians to judge it would not be safe or prudent for me to proceed on the voyage. Thus I was unexpectedly called from that service.

It was only later that Newton came to see this as a form of divine intervention. In the meantime, he was offered a position the following year as "Tide Surveyor" in Liverpool—a well-paid shore job in the customs service. This gave him sufficient leisure to pursue personal studies in the Hebrew and Greek of the original Scriptures. He began to wonder whether he was, after all, meant to enter the ministry—just as his mother had once hoped. Finally, he came to realize he must be "above most living, a fit person to proclaim that faithful saying that 'Jesus Christ came into the world to save the chief of sinners.'"

During his Liverpool years, Newton became a popular lay preacher. Though drawn toward the Dissenters, his deepest desire was to serve the established church. Several bishops, who wanted nothing to do with an "enthusiast" like Newton, flatly refused to ordain him. However, in 1764—thanks to the patronage of the politician and philanthropist Lord Dartmouth—he was offered the position of curate in the church of Olney, a market town in Buckinghamshire, about fifty miles northwest of London.

Here he was so widely appreciated that a gallery had to be added in order to accommodate the crowds who came to hear him. Together with his neighbor, the poet William Cowper, Newton produced in 1779 a popular volume of hymns later known as the *Olney Hymns*. Among those hymns was one that came to be called "Amazing Grace." Believed to be autobiographical in content, this hymn is today known and loved by millions worldwide.

That same year, Newton was invited by the wealthy Christian merchant, John Thornton, to become rector of the church of St. Mary Woolnoth, in the center of the city of London. Perhaps no one was more amazed about this than Newton himself, who later commented: "That one of the most miserable and abandoned of slaves should be plucked from his forlorn state of exile on the coast of Africa, and at length be appointed minister of the parish of the first magistrate of the first city in the world is a fact I can never sufficiently estimate."

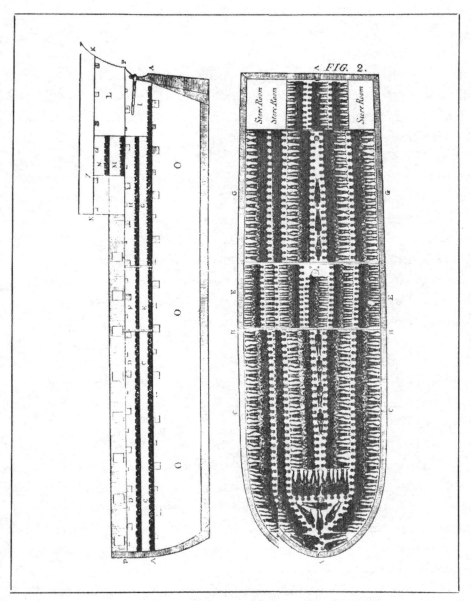

*Sectional view of a slaver, researched by Thomas Clarkson,
and used by Wilberforce in his campaign.
(Oliver Warner: William Wilberforce and His Times)*

GEORGE CHARLES SMITH OF PENZANCE

THE WILBERFORCE CONNECTION

Among the many church and lay people who came to visit Newton in matters of faith at St. Mary Woolnoth was a confused young member of Parliament for Yorkshire, William Wilberforce. One cold December night in 1785, he came to seek the guidance of the only one he believed could help him decide what to do with his life. Newton's unhesitating advice was to stand firm where he was—in Parliament, serving God there as both Christian and statesman.

Had Newton advised otherwise, the loss to the nation, and especially to the cause of abolishing slavery, could have been devastating. Small wonder some have referred to this meeting as "Newton's finest hour as a pastor." Wilberforce wrote in his diary that he saw that visit with the transformed slave ship captain as "a turning point in my life."

Newton's remorse over his role in the slave trade must, of course, have been well before that memorable encounter with Wilberforce. Later, Wilberforce could confirm: "I never spent one half hour in Newton's company without hearing some allusion to it." It seems quite possible that Newton was already thinking of his own moral awakening in regard to slavery when he wrote those well-known words in the first verse of his hymn "Amazing Grace": *I once was lost, but now am found; was blind, but now I see.*

The level of Newton's remorse was made public in 1788, when he published a pamphlet entitled, *Thoughts Upon the African Slave Trade.* This describes in graphic detail the brutalizing treatment and torture regularly meted out to the hundred thousand or more slaves who were transported each year on English vessels. The list of barbarism includes tales of merciless whippings, thumbscrew tortures, and throwing slaves overboard when they became rebellious or simply sick.

Newton began his pamphlet with a public confession: "I hope it will always be a subject of humiliating reflection to me that I was once an active instrument in a business at which my heart now shudders." His was not the only heart that would shudder. The publication was sent to every single member of Parliament, and at once became a sensational bestseller. Based on his own diaries as an active slave ship captain, it was the raw immediacy of Newton's eyewitness accounts that made his testimony so powerful.

Nonetheless, such evidence was not immediately successful in overcoming the entrenchment of the "white man's crime against Africa." The slave trade was at that time seen as a national economic necessity. Even a person of Admiral Nelson's stature could say that never would "the just rights" of his nation's West Indian possessions be infringed upon while he had an arm to fight in their defense or a tongue to launch his voice against "the damnable doctrine of Wilberforce and his hypocritical allies." During the two decades that followed the start of Wilberforce's campaign to end the slave trade, there were no less than eleven failed attempts to pass a bill to that effect.

Still, as Wilberforce endured the continuing loss of parliamentary battles, Newton did as much as anyone to win the crucial war of public opinion. He gave personal evidence in hearings before the House of Commons about a series of "butcheries and atrocities" so graphic that they could no longer be ignored.

At the same time, Newton did his best to maintain the morale of his parliamentary protégé. After the narrow defeat of yet another vote in 1795, Wilberforce was devastated to the point where he actually talked about giving up the campaign and retiring from Parliament. Newton countered that Wilberforce's reelection as MP the following year showed that God had further work for him. As Newton put it with great emphasis: "You have not laboured in vain!" The outcome was that Wilberforce carried on. Finally, on March 25, 1807, a bill for the abolition of the slave trade passed in the House of Commons—and did so with an impressive majority.

Meanwhile, Newton had, in 1790, experienced the grief of losing the unique companionship of his wife Mary. However, it gave him great joy to live long enough to hear about the passage of a bill that Mary, too, had so long looked forward to.

Shortly before he breathed his last—on December 21, 1807—Newton prayed that Wilberforce would live to see the abolition of slavery itself. Otherwise, Newton was convinced, it would become "a millstone sufficient to sink such an enlightened and highly favour'd nation as ours to the bottom of the sea." On July 29, 1833, three days before William Wilberforce died, he did, in fact, experience this victory. Neither Newton nor Wilberforce had, after all, "laboured in vain."

While serving St. Mary Woolnoth, Newton composed an epitaph he requested inscribed on the north wall above his grave. It reads to this day:

John Newton, clerk,
Once an infidel and libertine, a servant of slaves in Africa,
Was, by the rich mercy of our Lord and Saviour Jesus Christ,
Preserved, restored, pardoned, and appointed
To preach the faith he had long laboured to destroy.

With that last quote from Galatians 1:27—by the Apostle who "preached the faith he once tried to destroy"—John Newton points to a fundamental link he shared with another sailor. One who would one day also become one of the greatest preachers of the gospel—George Charles Smith of Penzance.

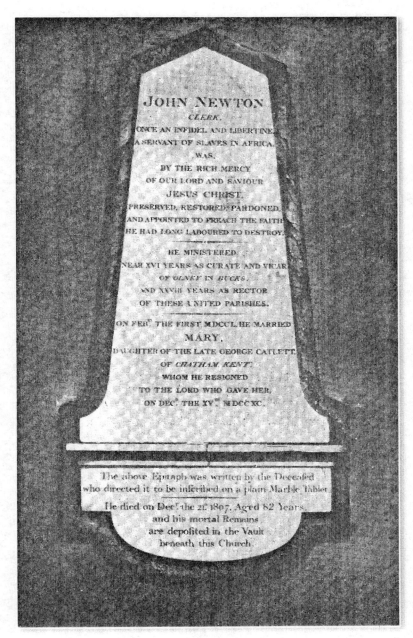

Newton's epitaph on his gravestone.

A PRAYER
(No. 371 in *Hymns Ancient and Modern*)

Almighty Father, hear our cry,
As o'er the trackless deep we roam;
Be Thou our haven always nigh,
On homeless waters Thou our home.

O Jesu, Saviour, at Whose Voice
The tempest sank to perfect rest,
Bid Thou the fearful heart rejoice,
And cleanse and calm the troubled breast.

O Holy Ghost, beneath Whose Power
The ocean woke to life and light,
Command Thy blessing in this hour,
Thy fostering warmth, Thy quickening might.

Great God of our salvation, Thee
We love, we worship, we adore;
Our Refuge on time's changeful sea,
Our Joy on heav'n's eternal shore.

BISHOP E. H. BICKERSTETH (1825-1906)

BIBLIOGRAPHY

LITERATURE BY G. C. SMITH

Smith, George Charles. *The Sailor's Magazine*. London: British and Foreign Seamen's Friend Society and Bethel Union, 1820–27.

———. *The New Sailor's Magazine*. London: British and Foreign Seamen's Friend Society and Bethel Union, 1827–63.

(Note: Also published under subsequent societies with which G. C. Smith was affiliated. The magazine's title varied over the years, from 1860 ending with *The Mariners' Church Gospel Temperance Sailors' and Soldiers' Magazine*.)

The different versions of G. C. Smith's magazine provide the main source of information and quotation on which this biography is based. However, there are approximately eighty other publications to his name. Among these, the following have provided supplementary information:

———. *The British Ark*. London (1817).

———. *The Boatswain's Mate* (seven parts). London (from 1817).

———. *The Custom House and the Bethel Flag*. London (1823).

———. *Aldermanbury; or, an Address to Mr. Thos. Phillips*. London (1827).

———. *The Mansion House; or, No Preaching in the Open Air*. London (1827).

———. *An Appeal to the Public*. London (1828).

———. *Birmingham; or, No Preaching*. London (1828).

————. *Portsmouth . . . Concerning the Admission of Females into British Ships of War*. London (1828).

————. *The Royal Brunswick*. London (1828).

————. *The Scilly Islands*. London (1828).

————. *Windsor . . . Prohibiting the Circulation of Religious Tracts in the British Navy*. London (1828).

————. *Intemperance*. London (1829).

————. *Persecution*. London (1829).

————. *A Sailor's Visit to Surrey Chapel*. London (n.d.).

————. *Bethel; or, the Flag Unfurled*. London (n.d.).

————. *Blackheath*. London (n.d.).

————. *English Sailors; or, Britain's Best Bulwarks*. London (n.d.).

————. *Injustice and Cruelty*. London (n.d.).

————. *Preservation from the Nore Mutiny*. London (n.d.).

————. *The Floating Chapel and the Sixteen Thousand Hearers*. London (n.d.).

————. *The Log-Book* (two parts). London (n.d.).

————. *The Mariner's Cabinet or Seamen's Companion*. London (n.d.).

————. *The Press Gang*. London (n.d.).

————. *The Queen's Bench*. London (n.d.).

————. *The Sailors' Hymn Book*. London (n.d.).

LITERATURE ON G. C. SMITH BY OTHERS

Blake, Richard C. "Aspects of Religion in the Royal Navy, c. 1770–c. 1870." PhD diss., University of Southampton, 1980. 213–15, 240–51.

————. "Burning Bush Unconsumed: Boatswain Smith 1782–1863." *Yearbook of Society of Friends of the Royal Naval Museum Portsmouth* (1987): 20–24.

————. *Evangelicals in the Royal Navy 1755–1815: Blue Lights and Psalm-Singers*. Suffolk, UK: Boydell Press, 2008: 231–37, 267–77, and passim.

Bibliography

Boase, G. C. "Boatswain Smith." *Reminiscences of Penzance*. Edited by P. A. S. Pool (1976): 70–73.

Boase, George Clement, and William Prideaux. "Smith, Rev. George Charles." *Bibliotheca Cornubiensis* (1878): vol. 2, 664–69.
(Note: See also p. 670: "Smith, Theophilus Ahijah.")

Campbell, George D. "The Sailors' Friend." *The Nautical Magazine* (1975): 283–86.

Down, Bill. *On Course Together: The Churches' Ministry in the Maritime World Today*. Norwich, Canterbury Press, 1989: 21–24.

Evans, D. Morier. "The Lamp of Life." *The Gentleman's Magazine* (1871): 619–25.
(Note: Part four of "Within and Without.")

Fletcher, Steve. "Special service honours founder of Seafarers' Mission Movement." *The Cornishman* (2004): 37.

Friend, Stephen. "Historical Notes: George Charles Smith, 1782–1863." *IASMM Newsletter* (1991): 11–13.

————. "George Charles Smith (1782–1863) 200th Anniversary." *IASMM Newsletter* (2004 –2005): 3.

Frivold, Leif, ed. *Vår arv: streif fra kirke-og kulturhistorie i London* (*Our Heritage: Glimpses of Church and Cultural History in London*) (1967): 26–27, 181.

Jones, Charles J. "Ocean Pioneers." *The Sailors' Magazine* (1876): vol. 4, 107–11; vol. 5, 129–34; vol. 6, 193–97.

Kennerley. Alston. "British Seamen's Missions and Sailors' Homes, 1815 to 1970." PhD diss., Plymouth Polytechnic, 1989, passim.

Kverndal, Roald. Interview with Leonard M. Richards of Madron, Penzance, July, 1967.
(Note: L. M. Richards was a direct descendant of Hannibal Curnoe, a member of the crew of the revenue cutter *Dolphin*, who in 1809 first oriented G. C. Smith on the Naval Awakening, which eventually led to Smith's life's calling. The interview was conducted in Madron, Penzance.)

————. "Memoirs of the Founder of Seamen's Missions in 1801." *Mariner's Mirror* (1976): 47–51.

————."George Charles Smith: Founder of the Seafarers' Mission Movement." *Maritime Mission Studies* (1998): 9–23.

————. *Seamen's Missions: Their Origin and Early Growth.* Pasadena, California: William Carey Library, 1986.
(Note: Materials about the life and work of G. C. Smith [documented with numerous notes] make up a major part of this nine-hundred-page ThD dissertation.)

————. "George Charles Smith: Founder of Organized Seafarers' Missions." *IASMM Newsletter* (2004): 6–7.

————. "Smith, George Charles." *Oxford Dictionary of National Biography* (2004): vol. 51, 132–34.

————. *The Way of the Sea: The Changing Shape of Mission in the Seafaring World.* Pasadena, California: William Carey Library, 2008: 20–37 and passim.

Lander, John K. "Seamen's Champion, or Unworthy Pastor? The Rev. George Charles Smith (1782–1863)." *Journal of the Royal Institution of Cornwall* (2005): 45–58.

Matthews, Edward. *The King's Brotherhood.* 1911: passim.

Miller, Robert. *From Shore to Shore: A History of the Church and the Merchant Seafarer.* Nottingham, privately printed, 1989: 44–50.

Mooney, Paul G. "Serving Seafarers under Sail and Steam." *IASMM Occasional Paper* (2000): No. 2, passim.

N. A. "Death of Boatswain Smith." *The Times.* (1863): 12.

Noar, Amy I. *A Tribute to the Rev. Geo. Chas. Smith (Bo'sun Smith), Founder of Sailors' Homes.* Warburton, Victoria, Australia, n.d.
(Note: Records her impressions of her great-grandfather.)

"Notices about 'Boatswain Smith.'" *The Revival* (1862): no. 179, 303; (1863): no. 181, 23; (1863): no. 183, 45–46.

Orædd, Daniel. *Sjöfolkets bästa bedrift.* Seafarers' Finest Feat, 1951: 54–55.

Richards, Leonard M. Typescript of "Minutes of Jordan Chapel, Penzance," 1967.
(Note: Relevant to Reverend G. C. Smith's tenure from 1807.)

Bibliography

Rosier, Violet M. Letter to Mrs. Hill. Kensington, London, 1936. (Note: Records her remembrance of her great-grandfather, Reverend G. C. Smith.)

Ruhrmund, Frank. "Simple but Moving Ceremony in Bicentennial Commemoration." *The Cornishman* (2004): 37.

Sailors' Society. "Bicentennial Commemoration of the Seafarer's Champion." *Chart and Compass* (2004): no. 4, 6.

Smidt, Johannes. *Fotefar: Spor av norsk kristenliv i London* (Footprints: Traces of Norwegian Christianity in London). Bergen, Norway, 1927: 62–64.

Smith, Theophilus A. *The Great Moral Reformation of Sailors, a Prospectus*, Richmond, Surrey, 1874: passim.

Stöylen, Kaare. *Arv og ansvar* (Heritage and Responsibility). Oslo, 1958: 147–48.

Trestrail, Frederick. *Reminiscences of College Life in Bristol.* London, 1879: 103–108.

Waltari, Toivo. *Finska Sjömansmissionen, 1875–1925* (The Finnish Seamen's Mission, 1875–1925). Helsingfors, 1925: 71.

Wasberg, Gunnar C. *Med norsk sjömannsmisjon i hundre år 1864–1964* (Norwegian Seamen's Mission through One Hundred Years, 1864–1964). Bergen, Norway, 1964: (9)24–26.

Wilson, Michael. ed. *World Mission on your Doorstep: 150 Years of the Seamen's Christian Friend Society 1846–1996.* Alderley Edge, Cheshire, 1996: 83–100.

LITERATURE ON JOHN NEWTON

Aitken, Jonathan. *John Newton: From Disgrace to Amazing Grace.* Wheaton, Illinois: Crossway Books, 2007.

Blake, Richard C. *Evangelicals in the Royal Navy 1775--1815: Blue Lights and Psalm-Singers.* Suffolk, UK: Boydell Press, 2008: 277, 281–85.

Cecil, Richard. *The Life of John Newton.* edited by Marylynn Rouse. Fearn, UK: Christian Focus, 2000.

GEORGE CHARLES SMITH OF PENZANCE

(Note: Marylynn Rouse also edits the *John Newton Project Prayer Letters*, published bimonthly since 2005 at Stratford-on-Avon, UK.)

Hindmarsh, Bruce. *The Life and Spirituality of John Newton*. Vancouver, BC: Regent College Publishing, 2003.

(Note: Containing Newton's book *An Authentic Narrative*, first published 1764, and his *Spiritual Letters on Growth in Grace*, first published in 1772.)

———, ed. *The Works of John Newton*. Edinburgh: Thomas Nelson, 1985.

(Note: A reprint of works originally published in 1808.)

Kverndal, Roald. *Seamen's Missions: Their Origin and Early Growth*. Pasadena, California: William Carey Library, 1986: 9, 16, 46, 79.

Pollock, John. *Newton: the Liberator*. Eastbourne, UK: Kingways Publications, 2000.

(Note: Formerly entitled *Amazing Grace: John Newton's Story*.)

INDEX

Index

SCRIPTURE INDEX